Hope & Healing

in Marriage

Also by the Author

Your Forever Friend:

A Tribute to Preston Hipp

Living on Jesus Street,

where the Mundane Meets the Divine

https://livingonjesusstreet.com/

Hope & Healing in Marriage

True Stories of Renewed Love

Updated with Discussion Questions

Pringle Franklin

Published by

Jesus Street Press

Charleston, S.C.

USA and Paris,

France

copyright 2015 &

2020

Pringle Franklin

ISBN-13: 9780692501238 (Custom)

ISBN-10: 0692501231

Library of Congress Control Number: TXu 1-920-97

DEDICATION

This book is dedicated to *God,*

the source of all

love,

and to the brave couples

featured here

And where does Love go, when the winds blow?

Detail from "Angels Restraining the Four Winds"
by Albrecht Durer, 1528
German Woodcut/Public Domain/The Metropolitan Museum of Art

Table of Contents

Let your fountain be blessed,
and rejoice in the wife of your youth:
a lovely hind, a graceful doe.
Let her affection fill you at all times with delight,
be infatuated always with her love.

Proverbs 5:18-19

A Gardener's Guide to Growing Love

1. Water the flowers! Enjoy physical intimacy several times a week. Do not let sexual frustration build into a barrier. Men, if you work hard to please your wife, she will respond warmly to your overtures.

2. Apply "Miracle Grow" generously. Men, be kind to your wife. Compliment her efforts on your behalf, as well as her appearance. Be sincere as you look for ways to affirm her. Women, respect your husband. Seek out and value his opinions. Refrain from belittling or constantly criticizing him. Praise him when he helps out or fixes something around the house. Don't keep a running score of who changed the last diaper.

3. Pull out the weeds. Daily. Women, stop nagging your husband. When you need something done, establish a mutually acceptable deadline from the get-go, then leave the job in his capable hands. Don't mention the task again unless the deadline passes. Men, do not patronize your wife. It may build up your ego to talk down to her, but this will cause her pain and diminish the flow of feminine love.

4. Spend time appreciating your garden. Husbands and wives should set aside time to enjoy one another. At least once a day, sit down face-to-face to catch up. Tune into your spouse and really listen. At least once a week, eat a pleasant meal together by yourselves – without phones or distracting devices. At least once a year, get away together, doing activities you both find exciting or relaxing.

PREFACE

In the summer of 2011, I dreamt I was dead. A man in casual work clothes appeared at my side. He looked like a guy who might pop over to fix a leak in the kitchen faucet. Yet instead of pulling out a plumber's wrench, he told me that he was taking me on — to the next place.

Yikes! Would that be the place of blissful salvation or the place of burning damnation? I managed to squeak out.

My guide did not answer. He would provide no information, no context. His face remained unreadable, yet he offered a brief nod that seemed meant to reassure me. I started to relax until I wondered: is he tricking me? Aloofness makes me uneasy. In South Carolina where I come from, we dive headfirst into friendly conversations in random places like the produce section. "Can you believe these beautiful tomatoes? Grown right here on Johns Island! The best in the South."

We are warm and helpful folks, even if we might be headed to -- but no. That was simply not possible. Why not? Because I love, love, love Jesus. He is the best thing ever (*ever* as in, since before the concept of time). Upon my death, surely Jesus would verify my heavenly citizenship at the window of St. Peter's immigration booth. Passport issued; entrance granted. Next! Full of relief, I would dash out of the queue and skip through the Pearly Gates.

But neither St. Peter nor Jesus was in sight. Who exactly was this guy? He couldn't be an angel; he certainly wasn't glowing, and he didn't have wings. Perhaps he was an elevator operator from the spiritual world, and he had confused me with another soul who had died simultaneously. It would be an easy enough mistake to make, like a hired driver picking up the wrong party at LaGuardia Airport and trying to take them to the Bronx instead of Fifth Avenue.

I wanted to blurt out objections, but something hindered my ability to speak. I felt pressure on my chest, as if my escort were using the force of his will to repress my voice.

I wasn't sure I liked this conductor. He was maneuvering in a zone where he knew the ground rules, and I was uninformed; everything was perplexing. By silencing me, he avoided the anxious flutters of my concerns, now left unspoken. That way he managed to keep things moving along.

With efficient motion, he led me to an empty space, a place of blank whiteness. Where were we -- inside? Outside? On a cloud? The only recognizable thing in this formless landscape was a spindly elevator. Frankly, it looked a bit vintage to be the famed Stairway to Heaven. I mean, the last time I saw a lift this rickety, it was shaking its way from landing to landing in a 19th-century apartment building in Paris. This narrow *ascenseur* looked equally confining.

Yet my silent guide held open the caged door, gesturing for me to go first, and I wasn't clear whether this conveyance was going up or going down. My survival instinct kept me back. That door might swing shut and lock behind me. Reluctant to move, I peered into the shadowed box. Might I take the stairs?

"You know," I said, somehow recovering my voice, "I am not trying to be difficult, but I am surprised that this happened so soon…I didn't realize it was my time."

The elevator operator looked startled, then slightly annoyed, but quickly he suppressed his emotions back to flatness. He pivoted away from me and whipped a walkie-talkie from his pocket. After mumbling something into the speaker, he received an immediate reply. I got the sense that someone important was on the other end. The guide listened carefully before turning to gaze at me with a newfound respect.

"He says you can go back, if…."

"If?"

"If you will write."

I did not need to be told who He was. A warm sense of surprise flooded through me in electromagnetic waves. God wanted me to write? He had more for me to do?

"Yes, of course," I declared. "I will. I would love to."

The next thing I knew, the man and the lift had disappeared, and I was set adrift in the nothingness of blanketed quiet. Peace surrounded me for several moments until a strong wind blew through and whipped me around like a dried leaf. Rather briskly, I reentered the physical sphere: I felt my body shake as my soul plunged back inside its mortal shell. My eyes opened slowly. I was resting under my bedcovers in the predawn darkness, rigid and extremely alert. My travels felt like a dream and yet, every detail was vividly etched in my mind.

My life had changed forever: now I understood. Christian writing was my new path.

Newspaper reporting had been my career before children. As a journalist, I had been trained to keep my personal beliefs separate from my professional work. I did not wish to be labeled as a Christian writer. That would soon change. I had received a new assignment — from the top.

Where to begin? My new assignments editor hadn't been specific, but I knew I had to obey. Reconsidering my priorities, I rearranged my schedule to create more writing hours in my week. When God reveals an objective (i.e.: write faith stories), often He only shows us the first step. We must simply begin, trusting that He will give us the next clue when we need it.

In my new office hours, I started working on a collection of wisdom essays. Just to get the juices flowing, I crafted lessons from life that I could pass on to my children, my nieces, my nephews. This seemed worthwhile, and I kept at it for about four months, but I felt there was more to come. Then I remembered.

Several years earlier, I had heard Melinda speak at St. Philip's Church in my hometown of Charleston. Vivacious and funny, Melinda told a female audience how God had helped her fall back in love with her husband. A number of twists and turns made hers a surprising and riveting story.

As Melinda spoke, I felt in my bones that one day I was going to write about her. Afterwards I introduced myself as a journalist interested in her tale; I told her I would be in touch. But my life was busy, and I never got around to contacting her. (Remember, this was before the dream that changed everything.)

Now I knew where to begin. Melinda wasn't the only one with a fascinating faith story; other gems were hiding out there, just waiting to be mined. I decided to write a non-fiction book illustrating divine healing from perils like cancer, addiction, adultery, violence, mental illness, or crime. Naturally I needed to pray seriously about the project; I asked God to guide me to the right people, the exact ones He wanted featured in the collection. Before long, the second story presented itself.

I recognized it immediately by the quality, honesty, and unexpected coincidences that are the fingerprints of God. I got goosebumps just hearing the woman mention the basic outlines of the events. But I had to tamp down my excitement. This acquaintance had no idea I was searching for material for a book, and I didn't want to scare her away by being too eager. It requires delicacy to ask someone to open up publicly on such personal topics.

At this point, I had begun interviewing Melinda and her husband Rick. Things were rolling along. When the time felt right, I asked the second woman to consider sharing her story as part of the project. After much prayer and private discussion, she and her husband agreed. I was giddy and yet, I was puzzled. The first two stories were both about God healing a marriage. I was looking for a variety of topics. I would just have to avoid marriage stories in the future unless — could it be? A light bulb flashed over my head — unless that was the whole idea.

Earnestly I prayed for God to make His intention clear. The only thing I was sure about was that I wanted to do whatever He wanted. After all, the next time I died, I wanted to receive a hero's welcome. *Just tell me what you want, Lord, and I will obey.* Before long, I had received an answer -- in print.

I was rushing out of my office to a small writers' group at a local Starbucks. Impulsively I grabbed my reference book <u>The Christian Writer's Market Guide</u>. This handy tool lists book and magazine publishers with a categorical listing of what they buy: romance, poetry, non-fiction essays, and so on. I wanted my writer friends to see it. We flipped through the index at the coffee house before reviewing each other's manuscripts for the next two hours.

In gathering my things before leaving, I swept up a wayward paperclip, randomly sticking it into the Writer's Market Guide. Back in my office, I flipped the book open to pull out the clip. By chance, my eyes swept over the page that had been marked. Right there, on page 54, was this: marriage/topical listing of book publishers. The paperclip had found the publishing houses seeking Christian books about marriage.

I almost fell out of my chair. "Thanks, Lord," I said, waving my hands in the air. "I get it."

Boy, did I.

In the past five years, a new separation or divorce had erupted almost every month within our social and professional circles in Charleston. The reasons were myriad: infidelity, emotional abuse, alcohol and drug problems, mental health issues, financial woes, as well as lack of love and emotional intimacy.

As a Bible study leader at our church, I had listened to many women talk about their private struggles at home. I knew that the time for this collection had come.

If you're reading this, you may be deciding whether or not to stay in a marriage exhausted of kindness, decency, or love. Maybe you despise yourself, your spouse, or your circumstances; maybe you are so worn down that don't know if you can hang on another minute.

Whatever your situation, these true stories of God's intervention are not here to judge you. They are here to inspire you.

Do not give up on God. His healing is not too good to be true, nor is it only for others. God is infinitely resourceful -- and forgiving. He holds treasures in His extended hands. Yet His gifts require surrender, and the cost of true surrender is different for every soul. Both the husband and the wife must release their fates into God's will for a marriage miracle to occur.

Free yourself from guilt; you are not responsible for your partner's behavior. Yet cleave to hope. If you are praying, reading your Bible, walking with the Lord and listening for His voice in an attitude of obedience, He will protect you and cover you with His love. That glorious covering, and the changes it produces in you, will shine before your spouse. You must continue to pray that he or she will bow down before the Holy One.

Renewal of love is possible, as you will see through the stories on the following pages. As you read, look for the points of surrender in each story and contemplate how these apply to your particular situation. Then focus on following God's word toward greater peace and happiness. This updated version contains Discussion Questions intended to facilitate study by small groups. We often learn best by learning with others who can relate to our pain and encourage our faith.

Remember, true intimacy in a marriage means you and your spouse share a deep physical, emotional, and spiritual bond. If this is your heart's desire, don't settle for less when God is offering more.

"For I know the plans I have for you," declares the Lord, "plans to prosper you and not to harm you, plans to give you hope and a future. Then you will call on me, and come and pray to me, and I will listen to you. You will seek me and find me when you seek me with all your heart."
Jeremiah 29:11 – 13

ACKNOWLEDGMENTS

I wish to thank many people for their help, especially my brilliant friend Betsy Cahill for reading the entire manuscript, and to Sarah Hemingway and Kerri Yates for guiding me through the early chapters. Each of these gifted editors has brought forth immeasurable wisdom. Additional thanks are due to Julie Chapman, Aaron Lehman, and Jennifer Whittle for sharing valuable insights. Kudos to Amanda Turner for the cover art and to LaVonne Marshall for the original cover. Lastly, I wish to thank my husband, Sam, for consistently encouraging me as a writer, and for putting up with me and loving me throughout life's journey. Below, together in France, November 2015, on the coast of Brittany.

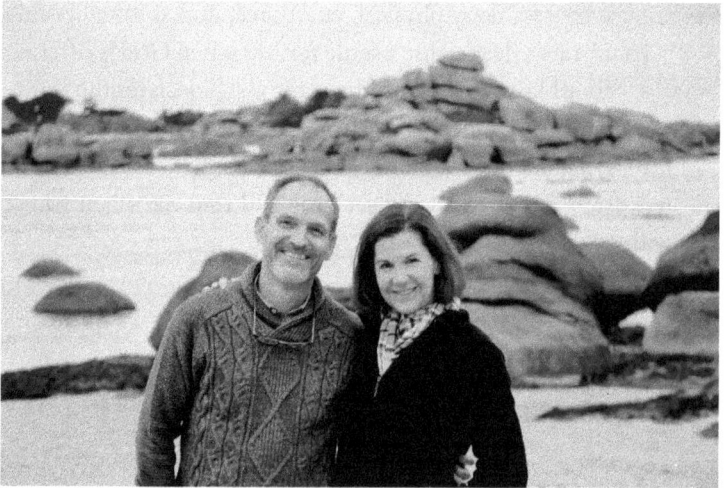

AUTHOR'S NOTE

Months of prayer went into the making of this book. I was dependent on the Lord to introduce me to the people whose stories would be in the collection. To ensure privacy for the couples, I have changed their names. A few of the place names have been switched as well, but in those cases, the general geographic settings were retained.

The updated version contains Group Discussion questions. Bible study or adult Sunday classes should encourage members to read the week's chapter prior to the meeting. During class, it helps for the leader to recruit volunteers to read some relevant sections aloud before answering a batch of related questions. This will add drama to the session and should illicit a livelier reaction from participants.

The last two chapters are told from a first-person point of view, as the narrators desired to share their stories in this manner. Although Hope & Healing is meant to encourage couples to hang in there, sometimes that is just not possible. It takes two willing partners to save a relationship. The final chapter shows God's mercy in helping to heal and rebuild a woman's heart after her unwanted divorce.

Please feel free to share your thoughts about the book on our Facebook page: Hope & Healing in Marriage. Or visit our blog for Christian interviews and inspirational stories at **Living on Jesus Street**. We would love to hear from you.

CHAPTER $O\!N\!E$ /Rose-Colored Glasses

"She was always comparing me to him."

Mariel & Bob married Jan. 5, 1980

The soft silk kissed her shoulders as Mariel slipped into her green evening gown. Her fingers shook slightly as she fumbled with the clasp of her pearl choker. Finally, the difficult hook fell into place. Exhaling loudly, Mariel pushed into her white heels before surveying herself in the full-length mirror. Yes, the three-inch stilettos showed off her curves.

Would Greg notice? Mariel inspected her image hopefully, trying to see herself through the eyes of her ex-boyfriend. She twisted and craned her neck to view her backside. The knee-length dress flaunted her tanned legs and shapely calves. Good! She swiveled, scanning her front for a final survey. Short, raven hair framed a perky, heart-shaped face. With black doe eyes, flawless olive skin and an engaging smile, Mariel knew she was pretty. Yet tonight, pretty wasn't potent enough. She needed to land a knock-out punch. Mariel smiled with pursed lips at her reflection.

She was ready for her 10th high school reunion dance. Now she needed to focus on Bob. With feminine precision, Mariel unleashed her finely honed grooming skills on her rugged New Mexican husband. She dressed Bob in a pinstriped gray suit to give the illusion of length to his stocky build. His dark hair, usually flattened under his John Deere baseball cap, now lay in slick submission to hair gel, magically transforming him with a polished Wall Street look.

Bob stood patiently as Mariel scanned his outfit: the green tie and pocket handkerchief ensemble echoed the tones of her dress. And on his feet, instead of his usual cracked and muddy cowboy boots, Bob had agreed to wear the gleaming black loafers that

1

pinched his toes.

Mariel nodded: Bob looked sharp. Sensing her pleasure, Bob grinned. He had no idea of his wife's real agenda: she wanted to make sure her husband held up well when compared to Greg, her dashing high school sweetheart. Bob knew Mariel's former boyfriend would be at the dance. "I was looking forward to meeting the guy," Bob said.

As they headed toward the door, Bob surprised Mariel with a corsage of white baby roses, tenderly slipping it over her wrist. Thrifty by nature, Bob scoffed at the expense of flowers. Even Mother's Day cards seemed like a waste of money. Yet this reunion dance was important to his 28-year-old wife, and Bob was proud to be the escort of the prettiest darn girl in all of New Mexico. Mariel hugged Bob in quiet thanks, drawing courage from the clean, familiar scent of him.

Mariel was uncharacteristically quiet during the drive to the garish casino hotel on the outskirts of Albuquerque. When they arrived in their minivan, complete with two car seats and a scattering of Goldfish cracker crumbs, Bob pulled the car right up to the hotel's main entrance; he wanted to spare his wife the trek across the mega parking lot in high heels. Despite being frugal, Bob was thoughtful. Each evening as he walked in from work, the first thing he did was wrap his arms around his wife and give her an enthusiastic kiss. Mariel appreciated this affection, but now, as the flashing marquee lights popped against the night sky, her thoughts flew to Greg.

❀ ❀ ❀

Charismatic and popular, Greg had been the president of their senior class. In their final year of high school, they daydreamed of the happy future that awaited as soon as they were old enough to march down the aisle. Greg surprised her with a promise ring before leaving for the University of Notre Dame on a track and field scholarship. Yet as often happens, the high school sweethearts eventually drifted apart in college. Eight years had flown past since her marriage. Mariel had lost all news of him. Then, a few days before the reunion, an old school chum dropped a bomb on Mariel's world: had she heard? Greg had recently graduated from medical school. The discovery rattled Mariel: *I could have been the wife of a doctor!*

Mariel could envision him wearing a crisp white jacket, looking serious yet compassionate with a stethoscope around his neck. That white coat would flatter him. Greg was just plain gorgeous, a Latino with expressive brown eyes, a strong jawline, and medium-brown skin. Just imagining how the nurses would chase after him made Mariel grind her teeth.

Every woman wanted to snare a rich doctor; no one dreamed of marrying a geologist with muddy boots. Bob's explorations for oil deposits kept him covered from head to toe in the rosy dust of the desert. Sometimes she found sandy grit speckled on the lobes of her husband's ears.

Mariel felt like she had been tricked. In the throes of first love, she and Greg had shared a deep connection. What would Greg think of her now, a mere housewife? As the big weekend drew near, Mariel would catch herself daydreaming at home while scrubbing bathtubs or changing diapers. Her thoughts would conjure up cinematic scenes of Greg proclaiming his undying love on a windswept beach while ocean spray salted her lips. She had plenty of fodder for creating such passionate scenarios; in her spare time, Mariel devoured romance novels.

The ardor of her adolescent yearnings unsettled Mariel. Not long ago, she had committed her life to Jesus Christ, and her desire to please God served as a daily roadmap. How could she lose control like this? She was happily married. Wasn't she?

❃ ❃ ❃

The DJ was already blasting 1970s music as she and Bob stepped into the spacious ballroom. A handful of couples were grooving under the strobe lights; a crowd of men had bellied up to the bar, slapping one another on the back and talking loudly; a long line of people was snaking through the Mexican-style buffet. Mariel's stomach fluttered as she scanned the crowd.

Was he here?

And what did he look like at age 28? In a crazy way, Mariel was completely conflicted: part of her hoped Greg was still as darkly handsome and athletic as ever; but another part hoped Greg had become paunchy and bald. "Then I could just mark that off my list and say I knew I had made the right decision in marrying Bob," she said.

Friends waved to Mariel from a nearby round table. With Bob in tow, Mariel smiled and stepped over to the group while surveying the room. Where was Greg? She found her mark about six tables away, his height making his physique stand out from the clusters of other heads and shoulders around him. His back was toward her, so she allowed herself to indulge in a long look. Greg still had a full head of that luxurious black hair, along with his broad shoulders and slim waist. As Greg turned to speak to a friend, Mariel saw his chiseled profile.

Her breathing momentarily halted; Greg looked as good as ever. Her pounding heart and sweaty palms revealed the potency of her bottled-up emotions. It had been so long since she'd felt butterflies in her stomach. She felt like she was 16 years old all over again.

Greg did not appear to have seen her; he was shaking hands and exchanging greetings, moving through the room in a seemingly random pattern. After several minutes, Mariel realized Greg was working his way toward where she was standing with Bob. A few moments later, Greg feigned surprise at bumping into her. She smiled shyly. Greg shot her a rakish grin.

He looked outrageously good. A long-legged blonde was clutching his arm; Greg introduced his girlfriend.

Girlfriend? That means he's still single, Mariel thought giddily, then mentally chastised herself. Quickly remembering her manners, Mariel introduced her husband.

The two couples exchanged small talk. Greg inquired if they had children; Mariel asked about his medical career. Greg explained that he was taking a year off to train for Olympic time trials in track. So now he was an Olympic athlete as well as a doctor? It was almost too much for Mariel! If Bob felt jealous, he never showed it. Her husband's hand rested lightly around her shoulders.

Greg whispered something to his date; she shot Mariel a furtive glare before click-clacking away. Greg politely asked Bob's permission to dance with his wife. Bob gave a nod, then stepped aside. "I'll just go get us something to drink," he said to his wife, but Mariel wasn't listening.

Her tidy little world was about to shift. Greg extended his hand and whisked her onto the parquet dance floor. As if on cue, the DJ switched to a slow song by Earth, Wind, and Fire, an old favorite during the era of their romance. As Mariel and Greg swayed to the sentimental music, the crowd melted away. Gone were Mariel's husband and daughters; gone was Greg's comely girlfriend. Nostalgic feelings of affection and desire swept over them, carrying Mariel and Greg to a place where, once again, they belonged only to one another. Their reunion felt as natural as the return of a river to its ocean.

Before long, Mariel would be gripped by the trauma of having to make a difficult choice. "If I could have had them both, I would have," she said. "But you can't have two husbands."

❊ ❊ ❊

As a child, Mariel had lacked proper role models to teach her how to build and maintain marital love. An unwanted pregnancy had forced her parents into an early marriage. As Catholics, they had stayed together over the years, but their relationship had never been easy. Mariel's dad, true to his Italian background, ruled by masculine authority; to avoid stress, her mom went along with whatever her husband dictated. When Mariel was 12, her father took his wife and two daughters to New Mexico on vacation. While in the strange, red desert landscape, Mariel's father informed his family that they would not be returning home to Massachusetts. "Dad just sent for the rest of our stuff," Mariel recalled. "We never went back."

They moved into a rough, low-income suburb of Albuquerque. Most of the kids were Hispanic; Mariel had inherited the olive complexion of her father, but she was still shunned as an Anglo outsider. She had a cute figure and a pretty face; jealous girls bullied her in school. Playing the hero, Greg rushed to her rescue. "He tried to defend me when a girl was pulling my hair throughout the science movie," she said. "After class, he told her if you want to fight someone, fight me."

Mariel became good friends with her handsome defender. In high school, their friendship blossomed into the classic first love affair. Besotted, Greg brought her flowers, teddy bears, jewelry. What a welcome change from Mariel's father: her dad kept such tight reins on his money that Mariel's mother could barely run their household. When they were old enough, Mariel and her sister worked after-school jobs as grocery clerks. Her father expected his daughters to move out and support themselves after they finished high school. Their future was their own affair.

Mariel wondered: would her future include Greg?

After graduation, her beloved boyfriend would head east to Notre Dame while Mariel would stay behind in New Mexico to attend a state college. If God willed it, their love would endure across the 1,400 miles and six states. "At first, he'd send flowers and cards and we'd talk all the time," she said. "We were still really close."

Mariel prayed for God to bless their relationship, but her connection with God was more pious than personal. At age 18, Mariel loved Greg more than anyone or anything else in life. This devotion would cause painful squabbles several years later when, as a newlywed, Mariel would compare her husband to her idealized first love. Bob's parents had never quarreled in front of their children. He was unprepared to cope with their fights.

6

❀ ❀ ❀

Bob had grown up as one of six children in a congenial family. His parents had met at the University of New Mexico in Albuquerque, where his mom had been a cheerleader and his dad had played football. They married in 1950. Bob's dad became a geologist working in the oil industry. His parents put down roots in small town Farmington, N.M., attending the Methodist church and Sunday school every week. They lived frugally and saved for the future.

"I grew up in a superb household, with parents who really cared about their kids," Bob recalled. "They poured everything into their kids and into our family. I never once saw them fight."

Bob's family enjoyed spending time together on weekends at their riverside cabin. He imagined always living in Farmington, going fishing with his father and brothers or playing rowdy rounds of cards until the wee hours of the night. In the morning, Mom would wake them up to the tantalizing smell of brewing coffee, frying bacon, and buckwheat pancakes on the griddle. In high school, Bob was tough enough to ride dirt bikes on winding trails or to sneak a few cold beers with his buddies, but "girls scared the heck out of me," he says. He didn't date much.

After high school, Bob reluctantly took his parents' advice and started college. "I wasn't sure what I wanted to do," he recalled. After several months, Bob was restless; continuing his education seemed like a waste of time. He dropped out of college and set off to chase adventure.

Over the next five years, Bob would work as a laborer in the oil fields, round up cattle as a ranch hand, play at being a ski bum in the Rocky Mountains, and drive 18 wheelers for a uranium reclaiming site at the Colorado mineral mines. Bob experienced an epiphany at age 23. He was sitting in a gas line on the industrial uranium site, waiting to refuel his truck. Bob watched as a middle-aged driver ahead of him went through the automatic motions of gassing his lumbering rig. This poor sap worked hard, yet he lived in a shack, struggling to support his wife and kids on a meager salary.

"I thought, if I don't watch it, I'm going to end up being him in 20 to 30 years," Bob thought.

Later that day, Bob surprised his father with a phone call, saying he wanted to give college another go. His dad made a few phone calls of his own and got the process started; before long, Bob was enrolled in the geology program at New Mexico State. In a boring philosophy class that he was required to take, Bob would meet the love of his life.

❈ ❈ ❈

About 200 students showed up the first day, and Bob planted himself in the last row of the auditorium. Soon his prospects improved. "There was a pretty little girl sitting down front, and I got my eye on her early on," he said. "She had the prettiest neck."

Intrigued, Bob worked his way closer and closer. After several weeks, he managed to capture the seat next to the main attraction. Mariel hadn't noticed Bob or his steady creep toward her chair. "I started talking with her, and after a couple of weeks, I finally asked her out," Bob remembered. "We went out and had Mexican food. I was just smitten."

Mariel was less impressed; she called her cousin to chat about the date she'd had with some hayseed cowboy who wore muddy boots, jumbo belt buckles, and high-water jeans. "But he seems like a nice guy," she admitted. "He is kind of cute."

After only a few months of dating, Bob started talking about getting married. He was trying to lay the groundwork for a future proposal. Bob was four years older than Mariel. His work experience had matured him, and he was ready to commit. He knew he would never find a better girl. "I just loved her," he said. "I thought she was the coolest thing. And she really seemed to love me."

At this point Mariel was halfway through college, and she hadn't spoken to Greg for more than a year. Bob had no inkling that Mariel still harbored feelings for her old flame. She had kept the promise ring, stacks of Greg's love letters, and dormant hopes that they might reunite. Yet Greg would have to make the first move to rekindle their romance. Mariel was not the type to look up an old boyfriend. She fantasized that fate itself might contrive a means of crossing their paths.

Then it happened. Shortly after a star-struck Bob brought up the topic of marriage, the former sweethearts came face to face again. Mariel and her family were down in Juarez, Mexico, a party destination just across the border, to celebrate her sister's wedding. Mariel was poking around a pottery and jewelry shop when suddenly she caught sight of Greg's mother. Mariel ducked behind a large display of turquoise belts. That woman had never liked her!

But if she were here, then perhaps… Mariel discreetly scanned the rest of the souvenir shop. Sure enough, Greg's bronzed and muscular figure appeared in the T-shirt aisle. He must have felt her eyes upon him; Greg turned and looked right at her. Mariel's heartbeat quickened. She waved.

Thank goodness I'm wearing a flattering sundress.

But as Greg stepped toward her, a girl with a long black ponytail and a shapely figure trailed behind. Greg leaned over to hug Mariel, but his embrace felt brotherly. Breaking away, he turned and introduced Mariel to his current girlfriend.

"It was really awkward," she recalled. Mariel forced herself to make idle conversation, then pretended she needed to rush off to meet her sister. In reality, she had to escape before she burst into tears. She felt like such a has-been.

About a week later, Bob officially proposed. Mariel told him that things were moving too quickly; she needed time to think. She enjoyed being with Bob, but he didn't make her pulse race. While dating Greg, she'd been swept away by a waterfall of romantic feelings. But that was high school, and this was college. Naturally things would be different. Mariel sought her mom's advice.

Mariel's mother liked Bob. He was upbeat. He was kind.

He was hard working. This match would provide financial security and a sensitive, supportive husband for her daughter. That was far more important in the long run than youthful vistas of cupids, rainbows, and fuzzy pink hearts. She advised Mariel to seize the opportunity.

Mariel, 20, was living paycheck to paycheck, working part-time at a clothing store while going to school. After changing majors three times, she was currently studying home economics — not exactly a career degree. Maybe her mom was right. Maybe marrying a considerate, responsible guy was as good as it gets.

"I really liked Bob," Mariel said. "I rationalized it in my brain. I thought yeah, I can do this."

When she told Bob, "he thought he'd won the lottery," Mariel said. Naturally Bob assumed that Mariel loved him as much as he loved her. He wanted to run away and get hitched that weekend. Mariel held him off; she needed time to plan a pretty ceremony and reception. Sheepishly, he agreed to wait six months to marry the girl of his dreams.

❀ ❀ ❀

Somehow Greg had learned of Mariel's engagement. When he came home from Notre Dame over fall break, he called. Could he see her? Mariel agreed, then counted down the hours. Yet when they finally went out, she felt self-conscious. After all, she had a tiny diamond ring on her finger; she was engaged. Greg said he hoped her fiancé was a *really* nice guy; she deserved someone who would take good care of her. The unspoken words hung between them: that guy should have been Greg.

"It was kind of formal; all of the sudden, it was like there was a big wall between us," Mariel recalled. When he drove her home, Greg asked if he could kiss her goodnight. She consented, stiffening her shoulders and holding her breath. They exchanged a timid kiss that fell flat. Neither one said anything. Mariel slipped out of the car and plodded back to her parents' front door. She felt dejected, even mournful. The old feelings had never materialized. She wondered if Greg would call again during his break, but Greg returned to school without contacting her. They were finished. Mariel sold the promise ring to help pay her bills and went back to planning her big day. Bob's parents had given them a used car as a wedding present. Mariel took it to a carwash and threw out three big boxes of keepsakes from Greg.

She told herself she had moved on.

Over Christmas break, Greg called unexpectedly at her parents' house. He had tickets to a professional basketball game. Would she like to go? Mariel started to accept, but her mom overheard the conversation and told her to put Greg on hold.

"Are you crazy?" she asked her daughter. "You're getting married in three days. You can't go out with him!"

She was practically Bob's wife and yet — she would have jumped at the chance to see Greg one more time. Reluctantly, Mariel returned to the phone and declined the date; when they hung up, she and Greg disconnected their lives. Without sorting through her conflicted feelings, Mariel married Bob. She was barely 21 years old.

Mariel and Bob moved into an apartment and started the difficult business of learning to live together while finishing college. From the start, Mariel found fault with the little things Bob said or did. "We fought a lot," she recalled. "I think I realized what I'd done. It was like, oh wow, I'm married. Is this really it?"

Bob had never seen his parents fight; he didn't know how to respond. He wanted to make his young bride happy, but he seemed better at making her miserable. "Our relationship was either red hot or red cold," he said. "We were either passionately in love or passionately fighting. It was awful." When Mariel picked a fight, Bob tried withdrawing into silence. He hoped to boycott the argument. "But that would infuriate her," he said. "And when I finally did respond, I'd blow up. I'd punch holes in doors and things."

Mariel felt slighted when, after a mere month of marriage, frugal

11

Bob ignored Valentine's Day. When upset, Mariel would pull back and weep, saying things such as *Greg didn't think it was a waste of money to buy me flowers.*

"She was always comparing me to him," Bob said. "Everything was so idealized and so far from reality. I'd tell her you can't compare a high school romance with being married, paying bills, going to school, and living together every day. It's just not the same."

Several times, Mariel kicked Bob out of the apartment; weeks later, they'd make up and he'd return. In one fit of anger, Mariel threw their wedding album into the dumpster behind their apartment. When Bob found out, he waded in among the garbage sacks and rescued the precious pictures of their sacred vows.

❉ ❉ ❉

That first summer, Bob arranged for them to housesit for a family friend back in his hometown. He hoped they would benefit from a change of scenery. In Farmington, Bob expected they'd meld into the close-knit circle of his clan, but Mariel felt suffocated by the constant contact and frequent invitations to the river house. She needed more personal space. Bob's family felt rebuffed, and Bob was caught in the middle. If he had to choose, he would choose Mariel. He'd never loved anyone like this. But he didn't want to take sides.

Unbeknownst to Bob, Mariel was making her own choices. After about seven months of marriage, she and Bob were fishing in a canoe one afternoon when she broke the news. This time, Mariel was strangely detached.

"She says, 'This isn't working out. I want to get a divorce. I don't like this, and I don't like you,'" Bob recalled.

Mariel recalls saying: "You deserve someone who really loves you. I am not the one."

Bob was stunned. This girl was the love of his life! What would he do without her? Yet they did spend more time fighting than getting along. Mariel seemed determined; reluctantly, he accepted her decision. "I can't make you love me," he said. "Heaven knows I've tried."

Bob remained in Farmington, and Mariel went back to stay with her parents until school started. Mariel's mother — mindful of her own financial struggles over the years — urged Mariel to reconcile with her husband. When school started, Bob moved in with some buddies, and Mariel returned to the apartment she and Bob had shared; to her surprise, she missed him. She reflected on her mother's advice. Before long, she called Bob, inviting him to come back. He came running, still believing that they were meant to be together and that this time, they would be blissful. Until...

"We'd start fighting right off the bat," Bob said. "She'd be ugly to me. It was obvious her heart wasn't really in it."

He moved in and out three times within two weeks. *"Who am I kidding?"* he thought. *"I feel like an idiot. I really love her, but she doesn't love me. I just need to get out of here."*

Bob returned to the bachelor pad of his friends. Mariel asked him to file papers for their divorce. Bob began the legal process, yet he still felt like a married man. He tried going out with his roommates; he sputtered through attempted flirtations with girls. "But I just could not get her out of my mind," he said. "My emotions were a wreck."

Months of misery passed. One evening after he finally had the divorce papers back from the attorney, Bob drove over to his old apartment. Tanned and shapely, Mariel looked so pretty when she answered the door.

"Here are the papers you wanted," Bob told her. "Once you sign these, you will be free of me for good."

A few weeks earlier, Mariel had taken the top layer of their wedding cake out of the freezer and chunked it into the kitchen trashcan. No use saving that for their first anniversary. Yet now that Bob was presenting her with the divorce papers, he looked sweet and sad. She felt drawn to him.

"I don't feel like signing papers right now," she said

without further explanation.

Mariel told Bob that she would meet him the next afternoon in the Geology Department. Because Bob was a teaching assistant, he had an office there. He wasn't eager to finalize the divorce, so he agreed. *What was going on with Mariel? She was so unpredictable.*

The next day, a little before 1 p.m., a nervous Bob sat waiting at his desk with the stack of divorce papers. He'd skipped lunch for fear of missing Mariel. But now his stomach was growling, and he did not want to embarrass himself in front of her with intestinal rumbles. Making a quick decision, Bob popped downstairs to the ground floor to hit the vending machines, selecting a bag of chips. Snack in hand, he turned around just as Mariel was stepping in through the outside door. Her eyes swept over him. He felt frozen, unable to move. Mariel's expression softened.

"He was just standing, holding that bag of Chili Fritos," she recalled. "He just looked so cute."

Their eyes locked. In Bob's mind, it felt like a slow-motion movie scene where two lovers embrace in a fragrant field of flowers. "She ran over to me, and I ran over to her," Bob remembers. "She gave me the biggest hug. It was the most sincere thing I have ever felt."

Mariel spoke first. "I don't want to do this," she said.

"Neither do I," Bob said. "I love you. I'll do whatever it takes to make you happy."

Bob moved back into their apartment; that night, they conceived their first child. The good news thrilled Mariel, and she finally settled into their marriage. Her pregnancy went well, and in due time Mariel gave birth to a healthy baby girl.

❀ ❀ ❀

During the next few years, Bob earned his master's in geology.

Despite a drop in the oil market, he landed a good job sniffing out oil wells in New Mexico. They bought a three-bedroom house in Roswell that was just beyond their budget. "We couldn't afford to landscape," Bob said. "Our yard was dirt and tumbleweeds for the first year. But we made it work."

Mariel became pregnant again. At a prenatal class, she met a friendly, likable woman who talked openly of her Christian faith. "She talked about Jesus like she really knew him," Mariel said. Intrigued, she wanted to find out more. Mariel had grown up in the Catholic church, but there was something more authentic about the way her new friend seemed to connect to the Holy Trinity. Mariel agreed to accompany her to a Bible study.

"That was when I really got into the word of God, and I realized what I had been missing," Mariel said. Through the guidance of her new Bible study friends, Mariel accepted Jesus Christ as her personal Lord and Savior. Eventually, she joined an Assemblies of God church because she felt it was the most on-fire church she could find.

Bob was confused: "I was like huh? I thought we were Catholic." Several years earlier, Bob had converted from Methodism to Catholicism to please her. Now Mariel was hungry for a pastor who would explain the scriptures in a personal way that she could apply to her daily life. She longed for Bible-based teaching. Once again Bob went along to please his wife.

Yet Bob had never seen anything like this place. The church met in a shopping mall. The pastor had big hair and a flashy suit. Worshippers would speak in tongues during the service; others would faint, overcome by the Holy Spirit. Each week as the service reached a crescendo, the preacher urged the lost to respond to the altar call. One day, while Bob was sitting in a folding chair, he thought, "This stuff about being born again is true, and I am not there, and I need to be there." He walked up to the altar, knelt in prayer, and offered himself to Jesus Christ.

"I knew that's what I needed to do," he said.

Over the next few years, Bob's faith grew rapidly. At home, he and Mariel read the Bible and prayed together. At work, he started a

15

men's ministry during his lunch hour. Mariel homeschooled their preschooler. Every day when Bob came home from work, he told his wife how much he loved her. They seemed like a model family.

But as the high school reunion approached, Mariel was beset by doubts: would she have been happier with Greg? Eight years had passed since their last conversation, when Greg had asked her out only a few days before her wedding. She could not imagine what it would be like to see him again after all this time.

"I'd start thinking about him when I was cleaning the house; your mind can wander, just like when you are reading a romance novel, your mind can wander in certain directions...," she said. Over and again, Mariel prayed against her romantic ruminations. She memorized 2 Corinthians 10:5: "Make every thought captive in obedience to Christ." For extra protection, Mariel asked two close friends from church to pray for her. She sensed that she was spending too much time pondering her old flame. Then the reunion hit.

✿ ✿ ✿

During their magnetic slow dance, Mariel realized she had underestimated the danger of being close to Greg. When the velvety music ended, Mariel opened her eyes and drifted away from her dance partner. She was dazed as she returned to her husband. Greg blew her a kiss before returning to his date. Mariel spent the rest of the night catching up with friends while keeping a discreet eye on Greg. She tried her best to repress the old stirrings.

At a class picnic the next afternoon, Greg sought her out for a short walk. Could they have a few moments together, for old time's sake? Bob smiled and waved as Greg led Mariel away for a stroll. Affable Bob supervised their young daughters at play. Greg waited until they were safely out of sight before squeezing Mariel's hand. Next Greg confessed: he had never stopped loving her.

What about the devoted girlfriend? Mariel asked. Sure, she was crazy about him, Greg admitted. But he would gladly drop her to get

Mariel back.

Mariel felt herself slipping. Not only did Mariel share similar feelings, she was in awe of Greg's glamorous life: the medical degree, the Olympic games, the travel. As an athlete for Notre Dame, Greg had ventured over to Europe and other parts of the globe for competitions. As he described visiting fascinating foreign places, an unspoken undertone suggested that he would like to return — with her.

"If anything ever happens to your husband, please call me," Greg said, looking directly at her. His thick eyelashes and vivid dark eyes had always opened a door in her heart. Mariel felt her knees go weak. She was afraid of being with Greg, yet she was also afraid of losing him again. She didn't know how to respond.

At the end of the picnic, Mariel struggled to act casual in front of Bob and the children. In making their good-byes, Mariel wished Greg luck in the Olympic trials, and Bob shook his hand. Mariel maintained her veneer of composure until she and her family were in the van heading home. Only then did she reveal her distress to her husband. To his shock, Bob realized that his wife was upset.

"She was saying things to let me know that she wondered if she had made the right choice," Bob said. Bob reassured Mariel that he loved her. He reminded her of the years of happiness they had shared and of their blessings in two precious daughters. She seemed to settle down. About an hour into the three-hour drive, Bob and their little girls fell asleep. Mariel drove on and on across the vast desert. She sobbed quietly to herself, wracked with heartache at the thought of never feeling Greg's arms tighten around her again. How cruel to discover that her first love still adored her, now that it was too late.

Or was it?

"I was a wreck," she said. For the next few days, she struggled to return to her routine as the happy wife and mother. "I was literally in a stupor," she recalled. "I was walking into walls. It was like, oh my gosh! What am I going to do?"

17

✿ ✿ ✿

Greg called when he knew her husband would be at work. He'd been thinking. Perhaps she could move into an apartment in Albuquerque. They could start dating again. It could be like old times! For an instant, Mariel's spirits soared at the suggestion, but she held back. As a newlywed, she had cruelly criticized Bob by describing Greg as the perfect man. Over time her doubts about her marriage had dissipated like morning fog. She knew she was lucky. Bob adored her and showed his affection more readily than most husbands. How could she be in this terrible struggle?

"I loved my life, I loved my husband, I loved when I was with my girls," she said. Yet Greg's passionate pursuit had unleashed a tornado through her neatly planted rows of domestic contentment.

Moving into an apartment? She needed time to think. "I'm not ready for that," she told him.

Greg didn't press her. He waited a few days before he called back. This time, he suggested they meet for lunch in a picturesque mountain village just a few hours away. He was dying to see her. If only she would meet him there, then they could explore their feelings for one another. This time, Greg wasn't asking her to walk out on her husband, he was inviting her to sample his wares:

Mariel imagined herself climbing into Greg's red Porsche 911T and stroking his right hand as he worked the stick shift. She was wearing a straw cowboy hat to keep the bright sun off her face, but the hot rays felt wonderful against her neck, her arms, her legs. Mariel didn't care where Greg took her as his convertible raced down the two-lane blacktop ....

Greg cleared his throat, waiting for her reply. Mariel shut down her reverie; she knew too well how that afternoon would end. "I told him I couldn't," she said. "I couldn't trust myself."

Yet her hands were shaking as she hung up the phone. Mariel decided to search the word of God for advice. After all, God is love. She hoped to uncover a Bible passage to justify leaving her husband. Bob had been faithful, so the verse allowing divorce in the case of adultery would not apply, but there might be another excuse she could dredge up in that book.

"I spent three days searching the scriptures and praying," she said. "I shed a lot of tears. I was trying to find a loophole, but I knew I had no grounds for divorce."

Her mind entertained wild hopes of Greg materializing unannounced to spirit her away. "I would be cleaning the bathroom and I would envision that red Porsche pulling up in the driveway," she confessed. She yearned for God to give her a green light to jump into the passenger seat and flee, yet her Christian faith was a roadblock. She argued with God and struggled to control her frantic feelings.

I should never have married Bob. I was too young. I still love Greg!

Mariel felt like opposing forces were battling for control of her soul. She kept flipping through the Bible, scouring the comforting Psalms, the wise Proverbs, even the lusty Song of Solomon. Instead of finding an escape hatch, she read verses about the need for obedience. Obedience to rules such as "thou shalt not commit adultery".

In Bible study, Mariel had learned that the word of God is sharper than a double-edged sword, so she hoisted it up as a defensive weapon. Mariel memorized and repeatedly recited Galatians. 2:20:

"I have been crucified with Christ; it is no longer I who live, but Christ who lives in me; and the life which I now live in the flesh I live by faith in the Son of God, who loved me and gave Himself for me."

This verse became a lifeline for her. She would repeat it to herself over and over until she felt calm.

On the outside, Mariel managed to appear normal. She braided the girls' long hair; she cooked Bob's favorite pasta dinners; she smiled and lifted her cheek when her husband greeted her every evening with a gentle kiss. Bob assumed Mariel had put the reunion nonsense behind her.

"I was not losing sleep over it," he said. "I had no idea he was calling."

❁ ❁ ❁

After wrestling with God for three exhausting days, Mariel collapsed into submission. "I decided I would obey God and commit to my marriage, and trust Him to see it through," she recalled. "I trusted that God would supernaturally give me the strength."

Mariel felt both relieved and deflated. Also, she was afraid: would she have the willpower to stick to her position? The next time her suitor called, Mariel was doing the laundry. While talking to Greg and listening to his adorable laugh, she prayed for self-control; she asked for God's help to stay focused on upholding her marital commitment. Greg was telling her how beautiful she was, how much he loved looking at her face, when suddenly the washing machine spun out of balance.

Thump! Thump! Thump! The whole house began to shake. The floor vibrated under her feet so rapidly that she feared the nails might pop out of the boards. She could not ignore the racket. Mariel told Greg she had to run. Quickly, she hung up. Perhaps her abruptness did the trick; Greg never called again.

Mariel wasn't about to call him. She trusted that the breach had been brought on by the hand of God. The Almighty was not above unbalancing a washing machine when it served His higher purpose! Despite this, Mariel continued to pine for Greg's attentions and wonder: *is he thinking about me?*

"I had dark days of spiritual battle, I definitely did," she recalled, "but I learned to put on the full armor of God." Despite enduring episodes of intense longing, Mariel never questioned the correctness of her decision. She stopped reading romance novels because they stirred up her fantasies. She filled her life with prayer, thanksgiving, and Christian music. She focused on God and allowed Him to send her strength and joy.

"The Lord was my lifeline and my absolute survival," she conceded. In the end, her desire to please Jesus was greater than her desire for her first love.

Before long, Mariel discovered that she was several months pregnant with their third child. The news floored her. What if she had run away with Greg while unknowingly carrying her husband's baby?

"Once I found out I was pregnant, that really sealed the deal for me," she said. "That just really closed the lid on it."

As a final act of repentance, Mariel told Bob about the phone calls and her dire emotional battle. Bob was deeply hurt by her temptation— and outraged by the advances of the other man. "When she told me he had been calling, I was like, whoa, I've been asleep at the wheel," Bob said. If Greg dared to call again, Bob said he would let the man have it. In fact, if he ever saw Greg again, Bob swore he would punch him right in the face. Bob never got the chance because Greg had finally given up for good.

For a long time after the reunion drama, Bob felt insecure about his place in his wife's affections. "He's been through the wringer with me," Mariel said. "His heart was splayed open."

Whenever she saw that dismayed look on Bob's face, Mariel was quick with a kiss and reassurance that he was the one for her. Eventually the painful feelings faded, and over time, even Greg's shadow disappeared. Bob was able to feel at ease again in their relationship. Mariel regretted hurting Bob. During times of personal prayer and reflection, Mariel confessed that she had not given her husband enough respect. "I had Greg on a pedestal," she said. "Memories are like diamonds, they just shine."

Now, after more than 30 years of marriage, Mariel and Bob are best friends. They get up around dawn most days to ride exercise bikes together. They play couples' tennis, and Bob often attends her ladies' doubles matches to cheer her on. They share the easy, joking manner of two people who love each other deeply and securely. Bob still gives her a kiss first thing whenever he walks through the door.

After their third child went off to college, Bob splurged and surprised his bride with a large diamond ring. When they had married as young students, Bob had paid $600 for a rock he described as "about as large as a grain of sand". Bob had already upgraded the stone once. This time he was tripling the size.

"I want to show you just how much I love you and appreciate you and look forward to spending the rest of my life with you," he told Mariel. His eyes brimmed with tears as he presented her with the new diamond over dinner.

Mariel was speechless. How did she get so lucky? How did they get so lucky?

In gratitude, Mariel and Bob mentor married couples through a program at their church. They want to use their experiences to help younger husbands and wives learn skills to build a lasting love. "I feel we've got to share our story," Bob said. "If not, then what's the point? Sometimes you only grow through the painful things in life."

In looking back, Bob sees the protective hand of God guiding them over time. "The Lord was really working in our marriage even before we knew Him," he said. "We've always thought that we've been given a gift, and we just want to share it."

✿ ✿ ✿

⌒For Group Discussion ⌒

1. Why did Mariel find fault with the little things that Bob said or did? How did Bob respond to her criticism?

2. Why did Mariel leave Bob? What eventually helped her to settle back into her marriage?

3. Later, Mariel and Bob both came to faith in Christ. Despite this, Mariel entertained romantic notions of Greg leading up to her reunion. How did she combat this? Were her defenses effective?

4. What occurs after Mariel dances with Greg and later takes a walk with him? What does she wish for during the next few weeks?

5. Does it surprise you that Mariel hoped to find a Bible verse to justify leaving Bob? What does this say about her thought life?

6. An unguarded mind will persuade us that we are justified in following our feelings to get what we want. Consider Psalm 23:7: "For as a man thinks in his mind, so is he." How is a person's heart changed by giving herself over to the pursuit of selfish desires?

7. Despite God's warnings, why do so many Christians fail to be faithful to their marital vows?

8. When Greg passionately pursued Mariel after the reunion, what Bible verse did she lean on and how was it helpful? How did Mariel use God's Word as a defensive weapon?

9. Was Bob aware of his wife's struggle? How was this possible?

10. After Mariel finally accepted that God wanted her to stay with Bob, how did she expect to obey a command that was contrary to her fantasies?

11. What happened when Greg called the last time? Do you agree with Mariel that this was an answer to her prayer?

23

12. Even after receiving this divine help, Mariel continued to struggle with passionate feelings for Greg long after he had stopped calling. What did she remove from her life to combat her longings for the other man?

13. What finally ended the struggle for Mariel and displayed God's omniscience over all things?

14. Mariel felt the need to confess. How did Bob manage to overcome his hurt and forgive his wife?

15. In thinking over the entire sequence of events, what was the turning point where Mariel pivoted back to God's will?

Reflection

"Submit yourselves therefore to God. Resist the devil, and he will flee from you."
James 4:7

"Finally, brothers and sisters, whatever is true, whatever is honorable, whatever is just, whatever is pure, whatever is lovely, whatever is commendable, if there is any excellence, if there is anything worthy of praise, think about these things."
Philippians 4:8

Mariel's process of resisting temptation:
   A. Initial stirrings: she memorized scripture, asked friends to pray, and prayed herself, yet remained weak
   B. Decision making: Mariel searched the Bible to justify her desire to run away with the other man. What the heart desires, the mind justifies, and the will acts upon.
   C. Turning point: Mariel surrendered to God and chose to obey His will as revealed through the scriptures
   D. Seeing it through: during her struggle, Mariel gave up

reminders or associations that would weaken her resolve. Instead, she focused on God through frequent prayer and intentionally turned her thoughts to Him throughout her daily activities.

E. Divine help: when temptation returned, God showed up by ending the call

F. Hindsight: Mariel understood the wisdom of having obeyed and was grateful for God's protection of her, her marriage, and her unborn child

G.

Room for Your Thoughts & Observations

CHAPTER *TWO* / Her Secret

"I wanted to tell him, but a voice kept saying, what would that solve?"

Lynn & Paul married on June 8, 1991

*L*ynn regretted the affair immediately. Later, in the midst of the most ordinary moments of her family life, Lynn cringed as unwelcome images flashed through her memory: the urgency of his lips against hers, the unfamiliar feel of his large hands, the musky, ticklish scent of his aftershave. It was wrong, all wrong! Her wonderful husband had no idea. Paul thought she was the purest, most loving wife in the world.

She'd be folding laundry, running her palms across the child-sized T-shirts in an attempt to flatten them, when the ugly thoughts assaulted her. *You are dirty! Worthless! Nothing but a liar.* Guilt and self-loathing stalked Lynn, constricting her mind like a python squeezing her skull. She longed to confess everything to Paul, to wriggle free from the oppressive coils of her regret.

✿ ✿ ✿

The filthy mess began in an online chat room where bibliophiles discussed the classics of English literature. It was the early 1990s, and Lynn was just discovering the immense impact of the Internet revolution. She and Paul had purchased their first personal computer, and she was fascinated by the mysterious and sprawling world of the Internet.

Soon she was spending several hours at a time in a great books chat room; there she met Josh, a funny guy from the West Coast who

27

appreciated her insight and her wit. She and Josh enjoyed many of the same authors and, before long, she was penning quips for the literary group with him in mind: what would Josh say about this? Would he catch her reference to that? Things escalated. She and Josh began sending private messages. Whenever a new one showed up on her screen, Lynn felt the prickly thrill of anticipation. Unlike her husband, Josh made her feel special.

At this stage in her life, Lynn was vulnerable to loneliness: recently she and Paul had moved to Boston for his training as a medical doctor. She had dropped into a new life in a large metropolitan area where she had no ties or established friends. Her husband was consumed by his work, often dismissive of her needs, completely exhausted by his rigorous schedule at a prestigious teaching hospital. Lynn felt weighed down as she slogged through a series of cold and dark winter days.

Her secret communications with Josh created some excitement. Not surprisingly, the missives soon leaped from the discussion of books to emotional and personal conversations, and the whole thing spiraled into a cyber courtship: flirtations flourished, sexual tension mounted.

Lynn and her virtual boyfriend exchanged hundreds of notes and eventually sent photos through the U.S. mail. (It would still be another decade before people began posting photos of themselves on social media sites.) Lynn hid the photos of Josh among her books but, when alone, she often pulled them out to study his friendly features and his handsome, intelligent face.

On his end of things, Josh liked the way Lynn looked too — Lynn was petite, with a knock-out figure and an adorable smile. She was both pretty and sexy. Over time, the gravitational pull between them became irresistible.

They agreed to launch a lover's tryst. Lynn told her husband she was going to visit a childhood friend, then she flew five hours across the country to California. She could hardly believe that she would soon be face to face with her obsession.

When Josh met her at the San Francisco airport, Lynn felt the jolt of unhappy surprise. In the photos, Josh had looked intriguing, with hooded brown eyes and a rugged chin. Sure, that chin and those eyes were there, but somehow his total appeal was diminished in person. Josh's shirt was wrinkled, his waistline bulged over his jeans, and his brown eyes were offset by the dark circles of too many late nights. Perhaps he sensed her disappointment; Josh kept glancing at the airport floor. He seemed tongue-tied and flustered. Where was the clever correspondent whose sarcastic missives had become the addictive highlight of her day?

Unbidden, the familiar image of Paul's goofy smile and tousled blonde curls, his merry blue eyes and dark lashes, filled her mind. Lynn felt the impulse to rush to the ticket counter, change her flight, and zoom straight home to her husband. But after months of shared anticipation, she owed Josh a chance. Didn't she?

❀ ❀ ❀

Josh drove to the hotel where they had agreed to spend the weekend. As soon as they were alone in the room, Josh threw his arms around her and rushed into a French kiss. Lynn had been expecting this; even so, his pace felt too frantic. They had hardly spent any time together. Reluctantly, Lynn kissed back, forcing herself not to break away, despite thinking: *this doesn't feel right!*

Lynn tried to relax and enjoy the experience as her clothes fell away to the floor. Suddenly, she heard an authoritative voice speak into her mind: "Lynn. What are you doing?"

Lynn wasn't especially religious, yet she knew without a doubt that it was God Almighty who was talking to her. Even so, Lynn felt unable to stop the oncoming train. She allowed Josh to finish. After the flurry of sex, Lynn felt sick. Intimacy with Josh had been disgusting. She realized more than ever — she loved her husband.

For months she had been wandering in a dream world, imagining that Josh was her soul mate. In her deluded state, Lynn had justified her lies and betrayal by her yearning for a forbidden love.

Suddenly she was vividly aware of her folly. She felt stained.

For years, Lynn had searched for a Higher Being, looking in the traditional worship services of stained-glass churches, in the cosmos of the New Age movement, in the calm wisdom of Buddhist teachings. She was hungry, yet nothing had satisfied her quest for the moral high ground of absolute truth. Now Lynn had no doubt: the One who had spoken into her soul was the God of the Bible.

How strange that Lynn would encounter God during the primitive act of adultery. She pondered this mystery. During her most vulgar and despicable moment, at the time when she was least worthy of His concern, God had cared enough to call her by name.

Lynn cried and silently confessed her sin while locked in the hotel bathroom. If Josh could hear her sobs, she didn't care. She wished she could go back in time and erase the whole episode. Her regret was sincere, and in return, Lynn received the healing comfort of divine forgiveness. For the rest of the weekend, Lynn remained aloof. Josh sensed her unhappiness and backed off. Before leaving, Lynn made it clear that things weren't working out. Their parting was strained.

❀ ❀ ❀

After bumping into God, Lynn blossomed into a born-again Christian, the kind who reads the scriptures daily and prays at every opportunity.

She started attending a church near their apartment and joined a women's Bible study. Paul was puzzled by her sudden allegiance to Christianity. He had no suspicions about her trip, but he was trying to understand what had gotten into his wife. Lynn wanted to reveal her sordid tale to Paul. It felt like the right thing to do.

Yet whenever she prayed about how or when to tell him, Lynn would not receive clearance for take-off. An inner voice – whom she soon came to know as the Holy Spirit — told her to sit tight and wait. *Wait? Could that be right?*

Lynn felt as if she were living a lie. While she dreaded hurting her husband, she longed to get this secret off her chest and throw herself on his mercy. Why must she endure this torture? Rather than explaining, the Voice would merely reiterate: *now is not the time.*

In the end, Lynn would wait in shame and self-doubt for six years. She didn't understand why she should have to drag around this weighty secret. Was this some sort of penance? Did God intend for her to carry this burden for the rest of her days?

Yet there were forces at work in Paul's world that Lynn never suspected. Only God could see the whole picture, and ultimately, Lynn's decision to follow His voice would save her marriage. Looking back, she could see how He had been with her all along, even during the turmoil of her childhood.

❋ ❋ ❋

Lynn's father had been an enlisted man in the Air Force; they had moved frequently, and when Lynn was in grade school, her family moved to Guam. No matter where they lived, Lynn's mother Kitty resented having to scrimp and save, and she blamed Lynn's father, Leroy, for not being a better provider. Even buying store-bought clothes was beyond their budget. Luckily, in Guam things were cheap. For the first time, their family had a maid. Kitty no longer had to sew jeans and blouses for her three daughters. She could hire a seamstress to do the work.

Even so, Kitty kept her eyes out for a more successful man. She started having an affair with a pilot. When Lynn was in the sixth grade, her mom announced she was leaving. "My dad was always crying, and they were talking about getting a divorce," Lynn recalled.

Kitty was unsympathetic to her husband's pleas. The more Leroy begged her to stay, the more she despised him. Lynn tried to help her father. "I remember telling him to stop begging and act like a man," she said. "He was crying all the time. He tried to kill himself and got put in a mental hospital on the base."

After all the emotional tussles, her parents eventually reconciled. When Lynn was in the seventh grade, she and her family moved to California. For the first time, her parents started attending church. The Baptist church appealed to Lynn, now almost 13 years old. As a searcher for mystical truth, she was curious about Jesus. One Sunday morning, the organist was playing the old-fashioned hymn, "Just as I Am, Without One Plea".

The powerful music moved Lynn. The preacher was making the altar call, and a feeling of urgency was rising in the pit of her stomach. As if pulled by a magnetic force, she stood up and slowly walked toward the front. After a few beats, both of her younger sisters followed as Lynn plodded on trembling legs up the aisle.

Weeks later at another Sunday service, the three girls donned white robes. The curtains at the front of the church had been pulled back, revealing the Baptismal tank and a romanticized mural of the River Jordan. The sisters waded in, one at a time, a milestone in Lynn's pilgrimage toward truth.

Yet her spiritual walk would falter. Her mother's unhappiness would pull Lynn away from her new church home and the opportunity to grow in the Christian faith. When Lynn was in ninth grade, her mother spirited the three girls away to Las Vegas, Nevada. Kitty was hoping to reunite with a former boyfriend. The man lived with his wife in suburban Las Vegas, and he did not welcome his ex-lover's surprise arrival. When her amorous aspirations dissolved, Kitty allowed her husband to join them.

Their fighting only worsened. Leroy had been discharged from the Air Force after being diagnosed with multiple sclerosis. He had only a small pension to support his family of five. Needing more financial support, Leroy turned to his extended family in rural Georgia.

His parents owned a small rental trailer out in the country where they could stay. Leroy left with the three girls, but Kitty refused to go. She had also grown up in the rural South and had sworn long ago that she was never going back there to live. Kitty stayed behind on her own to try her luck in Las Vegas.

It was almost Christmas when Lynn's mother called sobbing,

begging her husband to come and get her. As always, Leroy capitulated to Kitty's demands. He made the long road trip to Nevada and drove his wife back to Georgia. Lynn started menstruating while they were gone, and neither parent was there to help her figure out what she was supposed to do. Even after her mother returned, Lynn felt both of her parents were oblivious to her needs — and to the danger of her new environment.

Lynn was 14, and a male cousin, around 17, started dropping by the trailer when no adults were home. Before long, he started touching Lynn sexually. Lynn was feisty by nature, and she managed to avoid being raped, but she felt damaged. She started staying away from home during the times when her cousin generally turned up. She would not discover until years later that, in her absence, the aggressive cousin had molested her younger sisters. Lynn's parents had no idea.

The problem ended when, four months after returning from Las Vegas, Lynn's mother quit her marriage for good. This time, Kitty took her girls and moved to a nearby small town, staying at her mother's home. Life became more stable. Lynn's grandmother would cook meals. Granny never missed a Sunday at the local Baptist church. Lynn's aunt lived across the street. She bought Lynn her first pair of retail blue jeans and made sure the family had clothes. Kitty got a cleaning job at a local factory. In her free time, she stayed out late, going to bars and meeting men.

"She just started acting like a teenager herself," Lynn said. "I disliked authority figures, ever since she left my dad. I thought all adults were losers." In high school, Lynn started drinking alcohol and dating. Being molested by her cousin had made her more careless about protecting her virginity. She began to have sex with her boyfriend. But she was smart about it; she used birth control, and she did well in school.

Through it all, Lynn remained a believer in the mystical world. She had a natural curiosity, and she explored a variety of faiths and philosophies through spiritual books and New Age music. Granny read the Bible, and Lynn would try to read her grandmother's Holy

Book. Lynn still remembered the joy of being baptized and, on some level, she felt drawn to the person of Jesus. But the Bible was confusing, and Lynn never understood it. "I didn't have anyone to explain anything to me, not even my grandmother, who would be putting her hand on the Bible and predicting, 'Y'all are going to go to hell,'" Lynn says.

Instead, she went to college in South Carolina near the beach. What freedom, at age 17, to finally cut away from her parents' mistakes and misery and from Granny's stern judgments. During Lynn's freshman year at the College of Charleston, Kitty gave birth to an illegitimate baby.

Disgusted, Lynn stayed away from home. Lynn hung out with a fast crowd. She was drinking, having sex with boyfriends, and smoking pot. Underneath her party-girl lifestyle, Lynn was filled with unease and doubt. She'd learned that she couldn't trust anyone else to take care of her or to make things right.

❈ ❈ ❈

In contrast, Paul's early life was smooth. He grew up with deep roots in a genteel Southern town surrounded by generations of family and a lifetime of friends. "I had a great childhood," he says. Paul attended private schools and moved in the best circles in Savannah, GA. His father was a respected doctor, and his parents gave Paul and his brother all the traditional moral grounding. Most Sundays, they walked the few blocks to their church. Paul served as an altar boy. Yet the aristocratic social culture allowed for generous liberty among older children.

While their parents attended cocktail parties, teenagers roamed around, looking for adventure. Paul and his friends started experimenting with beer and liquor when they were about 14 or 15. With fake IDs, the boys would sneak into the local dance clubs and bars. It was part of growing up, like going to school or going to church.

"I was a drunk altar boy on many occasions, or a hung-over altar boy," he recalls. Going to church represented an obligation, a tradition, something you were supposed to do. Paul acquiesced to his family's wishes, but he did not read the Bible or search for the face of God. Why bother with a deity who might interfere with a boy's fun?

Paul noticed girls from an early age. And girls noticed him. Blonde and good-looking, both a surfer and a soccer player, Paul caught the eye of an older high school girl who introduced him to the world of sex. He was 15.

❋ ❋ ❋

During his junior year of high school, Paul fell in love. Mary Beth was smart, pretty, and cheerful; she filled him with laughter. When he wasn't at school or practicing soccer, Paul spent hours hanging out at her house. Mary Beth's mother was a born-again Christian, and Mary Beth shared her mother's affinity for faith. In contrast, her father was a biology professor and outspoken atheist. Mary Beth's father challenged Paul to consider the intellectual arguments against religion. "He and his friends would talk about God...he was interested in spreading his gospel of darkness," Paul says.

As a teen, Paul found this new point of view startling yet fascinating. Over time, the doubts planted by these unorthodox discussions would carry Paul farther away from the teachings of the church. What's more, Mary Beth's faith kept her from having sex with Paul, and he resented it. Maybe religion really was a joke. It certainly wasn't helping his life! While Paul had not rejected the outward rituals of faith, inwardly he was giving into doubt. Mary Beth's father was gaining influence.

"He led me into an intellectual position of agnosticism," Paul admits.

When Paul finished high school and enrolled at a military college in Charleston, S.C., he and Mary Beth drifted apart. Paul flung himself full force into the brave new world, where he enjoyed meeting people in class and at off-campus parties. Sometimes he would binge drink or get stoned and philosophize with friends about life, morality, or Jesus. Sunday evenings, Paul attended chapel on campus. While there he met Baptists, who talked about being born again. Paul had never heard that phrase. He was still processing his intellectual doubts. One thing was certain: he did not want to be like those boring Baptists.

He stopped going to chapel. He didn't miss it. "I didn't really want my faith to make demands on me," he concedes.

Eventually, he passed through the shadowed doorway of complete doubt. "I remember lying in bed and thinking: man, there is no God up there," he says. "There's nothing up there. I was crying. It was like my dad had died, or someone you'd loved, who wasn't there anymore."

❁ ❁ ❁

By the time Paul met Lynn, he was just looking for the next party. Lynn, a cheerleader and gymnast, had caught his eye while she was dancing and cheering during the college football games. "She was so beautiful, I couldn't get her out of my mind," he said. One of Paul's buddies actually knew Lynn from high school and attempted to introduce Paul to the knock-out blonde. She said a curt hello and walked off. Her friend mentioned Paul another time or two, but Lynn wasn't interested. She had enough boyfriends to keep her busy. Before long, she had forgotten all about Paul.

Yet fate intervened.

One night as Lynn walked into a popular bar, a random cadet dressed in the blue and white uniform of the military college stepped over to her. "What do you call someone who has a fear of strangers?" he asked her. Xenophobia, she shot back before walking away. *What a strange pick-up line,* she thought, shaking her head. Lynn attracted a lot of attention; she wasn't interested in meeting another bozo in a bar.

Then her brain made a sudden connection: her high school friend had introduced her to this guy. Maybe she should have been nicer. Lynn stepped back over, and they chatted. Paul was friendly, funny, and genuine. To her surprise, they clicked. Several hours passed quickly as they laughed, joked, and shared a few beers. Before long, it was closing time. Lynn had plans the next day to go to the beach with a group of cheerleading friends; she found herself inviting Paul to join them.

At the beach, some of the male cheerleaders were practicing back flips. They made it look so easy that Paul decided to try it. Paul managed the first flip with a spotter. When he tried to land one on his own, Paul fell hard on his back and slammed his head against the sand. He wound up with a bad concussion and had to spend several days in the hospital. His former girlfriend, Mary Beth, actually turned up to see him. Paul was surprised and flattered.

But he was ecstatic the following day when Lynn walked in carrying a small bouquet. Despite his injury, Paul managed to lean forward in the mechanical bed and steal his first kiss from the *It Girl* who had long been his obsession. After that, things progressed quickly.

"We both fell in love," Lynn said. She had been juggling several boyfriends, but she dumped them all. "I had never had a stable presence in my life until Paul," she says. "You could just tell he was genuinely a nice person. All the other guys I'd dated just cared about being cool and putting on a facade."

Unlike Mary Beth, Lynn would party, drink, smoke pot, and she had no hang ups about sex. "She made no demands on me to go to church or to be a Christian," Paul says.

Paul was a vocal agnostic, yet he upheld personal standards of honesty and fairness. Lynn found this an appealing combination. At this juncture, she continued seeking answers in the Universe, in fate, or in destiny. Lynn enjoyed arguing with people about religion or politics. Although petite and feminine-looking, Lynn cussed like a sailor and was combative about her liberal beliefs.

"People were afraid of my personality," she recalls. "If I did not agree with you, I would cut you. I was a harsh person, but very funny. I would fight with people about political stuff."

Lynn was spunky, and she felt good about her status on campus. Paul knew he was lucky to have her by his side.

❀ ❀ ❀

To Lynn's surprise, her self-confidence plummeted after college. She and Paul were living together in Atlanta while he went to medical school. He had embarked on a prestigious career, but she worked at a boring office job. Paul was immersed in a rigorous medical program, surrounded by intellectual challenges and impressive people. She felt overshadowed by that crowd. One day, Paul actually told her she was dull. That hurt.

"She felt insecure and inadequate in that situation," Paul says.

Eventually, Lynn decided to go to nursing school. She'd spent long hours in hospitals recently because her father was dying a slow, agonizing death from cancer. Nursing seemed like a way to help people and accomplish something with her life. Lynn and Paul married before his final year of medical school. A year later, she completed her two-year nursing program. Paul's next training took them to Boston, where he endured a backbreaking but heady year as a medical intern at a teaching hospital.

This would prove a dark time in Lynn's life.

They lived on the 17th floor of an ugly high rise near the hospital. Paul was seldom home, taking call nightly. In the winter, the sky turned dark before four in the afternoon, and the temperatures were bitter. Lynn found a job nursing oncology patients. As a rookie, Lynn worried about making mistakes. Yet no one helped her learn how to care for the critically ill patients. She felt unsupported on every level. After work, Lynn went out drinking with friends at the neighborhood bar. She stayed there getting drunk, knowing by the time her husband returned home, he would fall into bed exhausted.

Lynn became clinically depressed. On her worst days, she would take the elevator to the rooftop and stand near the edge, contemplating leaping into the void. Yet something held her back.

"I could always hear what was my concept of God speaking to me that He loved me," she says.

Artistic talents ran in her family, and Lynn started painting to express her sorrow. As soon as she finished one canvas, she would begin another. Painting consumed her negative energy. "That helped get me through the depression," she said.

Lynn spent many lonely days in tears. Paul was so busy ascending the academic ladder at his medical program that he neglected to help with Lynn's emptiness. "I was not there for her emotionally," he said.

Eventually, Lynn quit her job. "I was away from my family, my dad had recently died, I was 25 or 26 years old, and I didn't know what the heck I was doing," Lynn recalls. "I felt like I was a loser and couldn't handle the stress."

Worst of all, she felt like such a burden to Paul. "Sometimes I wondered if he's was just so noble, if that's why he was staying with me." Paul's parents had instilled in him the desire to do the right thing, and he operated under a personal code of ethics.

Yet those traditional morals would only hold them together for so long.

✿ ✿ ✿

Temptations lay ahead. Lynn launched into the new frontier of the World Wide Web and discovered Josh. Lynn liked to think of herself as a literary snob. Josh was lively and intelligent, and he appreciated timeless fiction as much as she did. "We talked and talked," she says. "We would talk about books. He thought I was so smart." With Josh, Lynn felt exciting again. She hadn't felt this good about herself since college.

Lynn decided she had married the wrong person. She needed to rearrange her life. Without explanation, Lynn told Paul she wanted to leave him. She was going to return to Atlanta; a girlfriend from college lived there and needed a roommate. Once she was single again, Lynn planned to pursue Josh or other relationships.

Paul was caught off-guard. "I was just devastated," he recalled. "I was in such complete shock."

Crying and brokenhearted, he begged Lynn to stay, and she relented. She was surprised by how much Paul seemed to care. But before long, Paul's focus returned to his consuming medical work. Lynn felt forgotten again. That's when she hatched the covert plan to fly to California. Paul did not question the story that she was going to visit a girlfriend in San Francisco. He even drove Lynn to the airport, wishing her a good trip.

"Thank you, honey," Lynn replied sheepishly.

If only he knew what I'm about to do.

❀ ❀ ❀

At the end of Lynn's dreadful weekend, Paul picked her up at the airport. Lynn flung her arms around him in a bear hug. "I was so happy to see him," she recalled. "He had no idea what had happened."

Paul welcomed the change in his wife. "When she returned, she seemed happy and at peace...and she seemed really into me," he remembered. "I thought, this is great."

Paul was not suspicious. He presumed the time away had helped Lynn clear her head. Lynn was back in love with her husband, and she embraced her marriage fully. She kept off the computer, not trusting herself. She started attending church several times a week. Lynn applied all the energy and force of her outspoken, opinionated personality to her new faith. Lynn had confessed her affair to God. She felt the certainty of His forgiveness. Next she wanted to put this episode behind her by confessing to Paul.

"I wanted to tell him," Lynn says, "but a voice kept saying, 'No, don't. What would that solve? If you want to be with him, don't tell him.'"

Perhaps it was better that she waited: one month after her affair, Lynn discovered she was pregnant. "I was freaked out," she said. Lynn prayed fervently that her husband was the biological father. "I was so relieved when the baby was born, and she looked just like Paul!" she confessed.

Motherhood changed her: Lynn had a new purpose. She was often home with a sleeping baby, so she spent more time every day reading her Bible. For someone who understood and appreciated great literature, Lynn had often struggled to grasp the fuller meaning of the Bible. Yet after her transformation to faith, she felt she could make sense of it. She relaxed and let the Holy Spirit lead her in knowledge of the scriptures.

She also spent time in prayer. As the months passed, Lynn felt herself becoming less confrontational and more humble. Lynn understood her place before God in the universal pecking order, and she was in awe.

Paul wasn't pleased with his wife's newfound fascination in the Almighty. "I was kind of bummed out about it because it was like, okay, now she loves God more than she loves me," he says. "That kind of ticked me off."

At Lynn's insistence, Paul agreed to go with her and the baby to church, but he set up clear boundaries. "I will never be the kind of husband who reads the Bible with you, prays with you, or goes to small group with you," he stated.

❋ ❋ ❋

Six years had passed since Lynn's affair; Lynn and Paul had moved several times as he continued his medical training and began his career. They had also welcomed a second child into their family. Despite his many blessings, Paul was still resistant to Jesus. Lynn had stopped trying to convert him; she simply handed that task over to

God. She tried to love her husband with a servant's heart and be the most supportive wife possible.

Since her conversion, Lynn had changed so much. Before they'd wed, she'd warned Paul that she wouldn't tolerate more than her fair share of the domestic chores. Now, she happily cooked, ironed, took care of the children, and even mowed and trimmed the lawn. Her whole attitude had flipped. They were living in Texas, and her traditional Christian values were a good fit for the Lone Star State. Every day she was focused on becoming a more holy person, but Lynn's hidden betrayal continued to burn into her conscience.

"I was struggling with, when do I tell him?" One day, she even called Dr. Laura on a radio talk show, asking her advice about whether or not to confess.

"You do not tell your husband," Dr. Laura advised. "You never tell him."

Lynn considered the expert's opinion.

Perhaps Dr. Laura is right; why should I stir up trouble?

Lynn had no inkling, but trouble had already crept into her marriage and started spreading out a sinister network of roots. She was sitting in a large Bible study class when, out of the blue, Lynn felt God saying, "Now! Tell him today!"

The unexpected urgency unnerved Lynn. At this juncture Lynn was pregnant again, literally heavy with their third child and approaching her seventh month. God's prodding to confess was unmistakable, yet His timing was questionable. How would Paul react? Lynn did not want to end up a divorcee with a newborn and two toddlers.

"I didn't want to tell Paul," she said, dreading the moment where her very future would hang in the balance. Yet despite peering into a crevasse of fear, Lynn understood her part. She needed to trust God and obey. That is what it meant to be a Christian.

After Bible study, Lynn returned home and forced herself to dial Paul's number at work. When she heard his voice, Lynn started to cry. With ragged breath, she barely choked out that she had something important to tell him. Concerned, Paul peppered her with questions. Was she all right? What about the kids? At last, Paul inferred her meaning. "Have you cheated on me?" he asked.

The moment had arrived. She could hardly speak. "Yes," she sputtered.

"What? I can't believe it," Paul said, his voice breaking. "How long has this been going on?"

She offered a brief sketch of the affair, then burst out: "I've wanted to tell you forever, but God told me to wait, and then today He told me that I had to tell you." She heard Paul sob on the other end of the line.

He cleared his throat. "Lynn, I've still got patients to see," Paul said. "I'll be home as soon as I can."

Lynn felt so guilty. Look what her foolishness was doing to her loving husband. When Paul came home, the two of them shut themselves in the bedroom while the children watched television. He was crying desperately, but he wouldn't let her touch him. She begged Paul for forgiveness. She offered to tell him everything that had happened, to answer any question, but Paul only shook his head. He could not stand to hear the gut-wrenching details. Between tears, Paul took a deep breath. Lynn stood and watched him as he paced back and forth. He seemed stunned, unsure what to think. Lynn feared she had lost him forever.

At last, Paul stepped over and hugged her.

"I forgive you," he said. Feeling his arms around her, Lynn cried tears of relief.

Lynn thought the initial crisis had passed. And yet, for the next several weeks Paul remained withdrawn, keeping to himself when he came home. At night he sat in a corner of the den, brooding in his favorite chair. He completely shut her out. If only he would tell her what he was worrying about, then she would know how to help. If she could have read his mind, Lynn might have fainted.

✿ ✿ ✿

For several years, Paul had been cultivating an exciting relationship with an attractive female doctor who reported to him on a medical team. He and his co-worker had not transgressed beyond flirtatious banter, but things were heating up.

"I was very attracted to her," he said. It was against his professional scruples to have sex with someone who worked for him. That was a sure way to damage a promising career. As a secondary concern, it wouldn't help his marriage any either.

"But in my mind, I was spending a lot of time thinking about this other woman," Paul said.

In due course, his professional duties rearranged themselves; as a consequence, the pretty doctor was no longer reporting to Paul. She worked on another team. That removed a major boundary. After so many hours fantasizing, Paul was ready to throw aside caution; the time had come to take this romance out for a test drive.

Paul had an upcoming medical convention in New Orleans, and he had convinced Lynn that there was no need for her to come; he would be tied up in meetings, and she was better off staying home with the children. But guess who was going? Paul's crush, and the two of them were eager to finally connect. Paul had been counting down the days when Lynn startled him with her confessed adultery.

"I saw the irony of the whole thing immediately," Paul said. "I was in shock. Here my wife is confessing this to me, and for all intents and purposes, I am in the midst of having an affair. I'm just speechless, just numbed by it all."

Lynn's confession shone a spotlight upon his own dark longings, forcing Paul to examine himself. He spent days crying and being introspective. Paul felt depressed and empty. Even the prospect of his affair, once so appealing, now seemed like a trap. Who had he been fooling? One night at home, he was sitting in his big green chair, stewing over the strange series of events and just staring at the wall. He pondered the sum total of his life.

He'd tried out the party lifestyle; he'd traveled extensively; he'd pursued an ambitious medical career, earning awards and promotions; he'd experienced the joys and travails of family life. "I thought about how I'd seen it and done it all," he said. "And I still wasn't happy."

Paul sensed he was losing his way, losing the moral groundings his parents had given him. He remembered his childhood in the church; he remembered the unwavering faith of his high school girl-friend. When did he stop believing in God? How had that even happened?

Finally, Paul reached a conclusion: "It was me who was broken."

Paul needed a fix, and that fix could only come from God. Paul kicked his agnostic beliefs into the sewer. "I thought Lord, if your way is the way, I am ready to follow you," he said. "I remember thinking there is nothing else out there for me — this is the only answer I know. I felt this deep peace about me. It was kind of dramatic, really."

Soon after, Paul confessed his secret love interest to Lynn. She was stunned. How could she have missed picking up on this? She had assumed their marriage was fireproof. After the initial sting, she made what she felt was an obvious choice. *Paul has forgiven me; how can I not forgive him?*

After receiving his wife's forgiveness, Paul punted his pursuit of the other woman. He felt so free! Just as Paul had been madly dancing on the edge of a cliff, the Lord of All Creation had intervened to offer a way out.

From then on, Paul thirsted after closeness to God. He actually enjoyed attending church and Bible studies with Lynn. Over time, Paul established a lasting faith. As Paul looks back at this turning point, he marvels at God's wisdom. "This says to me that God's timing is perfect," Paul says. "Joseph says it well at the end of Genesis — what man had intended for bad, God intended for good."

Paul hopes their story can encourage others. "God manifests Himself in us through the relationships we have with other people," he says. "Marriage was part of His plan from the beginning. He said, 'I see man sitting there in the garden alone, and it is not good.'"

After more than 25 years of marriage, Lynn and Paul still share a passionate relationship. Lynn loves to dance to popular music, and

Paul enjoys being right there beside her. Anyone who sees them laughing and grooving on the dance floor can tell they adore one another. Their common values and deep faith serve as the foundation for their family. At dinner, they read the Bible and teach life lessons to their three children. But they also cut up, giggle, and share silly jokes with their teenagers.

"My husband is the greatest guy I know," Lynn says. "I am so thankful for God's mercy."

❁ ❁ ❁

For Group Discussion

1. What made Lynn susceptible to getting involved with another man? What did her cyber boyfriend bring to her life that was missing?

2. What happened when Lynn met Josh in person? Despite feeling squeamish, why did she allow Josh to seduce her?

3. What had been Lynn's history of faith? At the hotel, how did she recognize the voice within?

4. Why do you think God would choose to speak to Lynn during a shameful episode?

5. How did her encounter with God give her sudden clarity? In her deluded state, how had Lynn justified her behavior in establishing an extramarital relationship?

6. Remember: what the heart desires, the mind justifies, and the will acts upon. How have you seen this principle at work in your life?

7. How did Lynn deal with the guilt of her mistake?

8. In what ways did Lynn change after she returned home? What did Paul think was going on in their relationship?

9. Eventually Lynn wanted to confess her affair to her husband. What did she hear from the Holy Spirit whenever she thought about telling Paul?

10. Explain how this applies to Lynn: "Whether you turn to the right or to the left, your ears will hear a voice behind you, saying this is the way; walk in it." Isaiah 30:21

11. What is required for a person to be able to hear the Holy Spirit?

12. What did Paul think about Lynn's new devotion to God? What boundaries did he put in place about his own participation in her

religion?

13. What prompted Lynn finally to tell Paul about the affair?

14. How was God's timing perfect?

15. How did Paul struggle before surrendering to God? Why do people prefer to solve their own problems instead of deepening their relationship with God Almighty?

16. In thinking over the entire sequence of events, what were the turning points when first Lynn, then Paul, found God?

Reflection

"Trust in the Lord with all your heart and lean not on our own understanding; in all your ways submit to Him, and He will make your paths straight."
Proverbs 3:5-6

"And we know that for those who love God, all things work together for good, for those who are called according to His purpose."
Romans 8:28

How were these promises this true for Lynn and Paul? How might these scriptures be true in your life? Take a moment to sit quietly before the Lord. Visualize placing your concerns in the palm of your hands and lifting them up to God. As you release your burdens, pray silently: "Not my will, but thy perfect and holy will be done." Then allow your cares to rest in His hands, trusting God to untangle the threads and weave a beautiful design into the tapestry of your life.

Room for Your Thoughts & Observations

CHAPTER *THREE* / The Daily War

"She was just so angry; she hated my guts."

Melinda and Rick married May 1, 1994

After only four years of marriage, Melinda detested her husband. She practically despised every curly red hair on Rick's head. "I felt I would just like to grab him around the neck and strangle the life out of him," Melinda said.

Melinda was jealous of Rick's son from his first marriage. Cole, age five, spent every weekend with them. He also visited every Wednesday night. It wasn't normal, Melinda grumbled; Rick needed to rework his custody arrangement.

"Don't do this to me, Melinda," Rick warned. "If you make me make a choice between you and Cole, you're going to lose."

Melinda silenced her demands but remained resentful. She wasn't mean to Cole; he was too cute. Instead Rick served as the lightning rod for her wrath. She zapped him verbally, constantly complaining. "I hated the way Rick needed his son so much," she recalled.

Melinda's father, angry and abusive, had never cherished time with her during her childhood in Greenville, S.C. She had never experienced anything like this kind of paternal love.

Whenever Rick read a picture book to Cole, they snuggled together, both so contented. Melinda had never wanted children; she feared turning into an abusive parent like her father. However, Melinda was approaching 36 years old and was concerned about her biological clock. Her child-bearing days were passing her by. Was she making a mistake? With Rick beside her, maybe she could figure out how to be a decent mother. When she discussed it with Rick, he was delighted; eventually they had a son of their own.

Motherhood softened Melinda's view of her stepson. Cole adored his baby brother, and Melinda felt connected to him in a new way. He was her baby's sibling. That made them true family now. The Cole problem was solved, but soon Melinda had another reason to fume. Melinda dreaded leaving her baby after her maternity leave ended. She could not imagine returning to work as a hospital nurse when her tiny little boy needed her so much.

Melinda tried to convince Rick that she should be able to stay home like Cole's mother. Thanks to Rick's generosity when he divorced his first wife, Kim was a full-time mom. But Rick wasn't able to provide enough for both wives to stay home. Besides supporting his first family, Rick was paying off significant debt from his advanced degree to become a nurse anesthetist. He reminded Melinda that they relied on her additional income. Melinda cried at the idea of sending her baby to daycare, but Rick remained firm. Melinda returned to her job, and Baby Billy went to childcare.

She was incensed.

"It was like, this is war," Melinda says. "I started looking for ways to make Rick's life miserable."

"I just used to dread coming home to Melinda," Rick concedes. "It was like the least little thing would set her off. Nothing was ever easy."

Religious differences added to their unhappiness. Melinda was an entrenched Southern Baptist who wanted her husband to love Jesus. Rick considered himself agnostic: God might or might not exist in some remote way, but Rick felt certain that the divinity of Jesus Christ was a myth. "No one had ever been raised from the dead," Rick said. "I had never seen a miracle. Miracles didn't exist."

✿ ✿ ✿

Rick had grown up in a steel mill town in northern West Virginia. As a toddler, Rick would hop off the couch and plant his open palm on the T.V. screen whenever televangelist Oral Roberts held out his hand to the audience. His mother would laugh at her son's odd behavior. The family did not foster their child's spiritual curiosity. Rick's father, a mill worker, thought religion was a crutch of the weak. His mother never ventured to church.

"For us, Sunday was just any other day," Rick recalled. "It was the day the Steelers came on."

To their dismay, the non-religious family caught the eye of Father Redman, a young and eager Episcopal priest. Rick's family has a legendary story about the priest's irritating habit of popping by their house uninvited. One morning Rick's mother was home alone when she saw the soul-saving cleric getting out of his black Plymouth Valiant and walking toward her front door.

Not again! Just in time, she ducked into the living room and crouched behind the sofa. While the collared priest knocked vigorously, Rick's mother held deathly still, trying to stay out of sight. Finally, the knocking ceased. She counted to sixty, then slowly stood up and peeped around a curtain. Father Redman was standing right there, outside the picture window. He smiled at her and waved. Rick's mom felt forced to open the door, but she never opened her heart. Despite that, the priest continued to reach out to the family, and over time, he won some ground.

In middle school, Rick began venturing out to Father Redman's small Tudor-style sanctuary. Rick enjoyed the peaceful, ritual-based services at The Church of the Good Shepherd. The mildly perfumed candles and wood polish filled the sanctuary with a soothing aroma. Somehow it smelled holy in that little church with the wood-beamed gothic ceiling. At times Rick felt awkward attending church by himself as an adolescent, but Father Redman always smiled warmly and shook his hand, asking Rick about school or sports and making him feel welcome. The priest looked for opportunities to encourage the young man toward faith; Rick enjoyed their connection.

Then high school hit.

Rick was a good athlete who loved sports, and he started playing basketball, baseball, and tennis for his school. What's more, he began dating a cute blonde and fell madly in love. Before long, he had outgrown his need for The Good Shepherd. "I became much too cool to go to church," he said.

In fact, twenty-five years would pass before Rick would venture back into God's house.

He was too busy for God, and his concept of a Heavenly Father became hazy. Why did he need to pray? Rick had what he wanted: he graduated from high school, got a job, and married Kim, his sweetheart. They married at age 20 and planned to spend their all days living happily in the comfy confines of their small mountain hometown. Rick followed the expected path and worked for good hourly wages at the local steel mill. Rick was happy enough, but after a few years, he began to feel as if something were missing. For reasons that he could not name, a disruptive sensation of longing haunted Rick. Was he meant for something more than punching a time clock? If so, what?

No one saw it coming when Rick left the mill to attend community college in pursuit of a low-level nursing degree. The steel mill paid for the education, and Rick returned to his same old job after graduation. Kim was relieved; she thought Rick had put this nonsense behind him. His hourly job at the mill paid three times more than any nursing job.

Yet restlessness continued to gnaw at Rick's sense of happiness. On a lark, Rick applied for a nursing job in a sunny city situated among green marshlands and palmetto trees on the Atlantic coast. When Rick was hired, he threw off his familiar life — in a place where he knew every gnarled crevice on every rock face of every surrounding mountain — and moved off to the foreign flatlands of Charleston. He loved the idea that he could play outdoor tennis straight through the winter down there.

Kim was reluctant to leave their hometown in the Appalachian Mountains. In fact, she refused to move for three months because she didn't think Rick would last in South Carolina. She joined him in his new life only after realizing that he was not coming back.

As things would turn out, Rick would never go back to live in West Virginia. He continued working in Charleston while earning a bachelor's degree in nursing. He became a father after Kim gave birth to Cole. This new responsibility only increased Rick's desire to excel. He longed to become a nurse anesthetist, the top paying job in his field. Yet that would require him to stop working for 27 months to attend rigorous, full-time school. He was his family's main bread winner, so Rick started socking away money to pay for his dream.

Then Hurricane Hugo devastated the South Carolina coast in 1989. Rick, Kim, and young Cole were living in a rental at the beach; their entire household was destroyed, but their renter's insurance refused to pay out a dime. By the time the family had replaced their clothes and household goods, and put down a deposit on a new rental, Rick had wiped out his entire savings for school.

The timing couldn't have been worse: the local nurse anesthetist program had recently accepted Rick. It was now or never. Rick quit his job and took out significant loans.

Everything about his and Kim's situation was stressful: they had a toddler; their credit cards were maxed out; Rick owed thousands of dollars for his education. When he finally became a nurse anesthetist, Rick stepped back and surveyed his life. He felt his 18-year marriage was an empty shell.

"It was uncomfortable to know what to talk about when we were alone," he confessed. "I told her we both deserved something better."

Rick took all the debt with him when he left. He also took a load of guilt for divorcing his son's mother. He did not want to remain married to Kim, but Rick felt lonely on a primal level.

For the first time in decades, the church seemed appealing. A friend had mentioned a low-key Episcopal church at the beach; even the name sounded reassuring to Rick's bruised heart — Holy Comforter. When Rick knelt in the old-fashioned wooden pews, he found the rituals and repetitive prayers soothing, a throwback to his boyhood visits in Father Redman's Episcopal parish.

Despite his skepticism, Rick began showing up for the services; somehow, it was peaceful in there. He wasn't looking to meet God beside the stained-glass window; the church simply offered a calm, uplifting place to sit and reflect. Rick didn't want anyone to latch onto him and attempt to lead him to commit to Jesus Christ. The prospect of that unpleasantness made him squirm. Toward the end of each service, Rick would duck out a few minutes early before having to shake hands with the minister at the front door.

❆ ❆ ❆

Melinda had received Christ at age 12, under the guidance of her Southern Baptist pastor. Even as a young girl, she felt warmth and love radiating from her Heavenly Father. "I had a heart for God," she said.

By contrast, her earthly father belittled and insulted her, bellowed threats and slammed doors. Melinda never seemed able to do anything right. His taunts and temper besieged her. Melinda's mother tried to protect her daughter, but she was no match for her aggressive husband.

Eventually the parents divorced. As soon as she graduated from high school, Melinda escaped by going off to nursing school. She avoided contact with her father. He made no attempts to communicate with her.

By the time she was 25 years old, Melinda mourned the loss of a paternal relationship. Now that she and her father had put some distance between them, Melinda began to believe that they might find a way to treat each other better. She wrote her father a long letter, admitting her faults and asking if they could start again.

"He did not receive it well," Melinda recalled. Melinda's father saw the apologies expressed in her letter as proof that she was to blame for their toxic relationship. He said he did not wish to see her.

Melinda felt slapped down and foolish. Had she honestly expected him to change? The memory of her father's hurtful words came roaring back into her conscious thoughts. He still had power to torment her. Melinda didn't know how to find release from the pain and self-doubt. She shoved her damaged feelings to the bottom of her soul.

Melinda refused to think about her father. She would not allow him to ruin her life. Instead she coped by covering up with a happy face. By nature, Melinda was a vivacious extrovert, so she hid her scars behind humor and perky chatter.

"It was like, just keep laughing, because if you stop too long, you might have to think about things, and I was not prepared to do that," Melinda conceded.

After Melinda graduated from nursing school, she began working as a nurse in a hospital near Charleston. There she met Rick, also a nurse. He was quiet, solid, reliable. Rick was married, but he and Melinda were friendly. Melinda fell in love with Jock, another male nurse, and eventually they wed. Jock wanted children, but Melinda refused. She feared she would morph into a copycat of her abusive father. She wasn't willing to dig through her past in order to overcome it. She told herself that she had moved on.

Unknown to Melinda, dark clouds were gathering across her emotional horizon: one summer day, her father drowned in a freak accident while fishing during a vacation. Melinda was stunned. Four years earlier, her father had refused to reconcile after receiving her letter. Now his sudden death obliterated any chance of ever making amends. Once again, Melinda repressed the hurt, but it festered.

Within two years, her marriage to Jock had soured. Any little thing could set her off; Melinda constantly criticized Jock and insulted him, much as her father had done to her.

"I had all this pent-up resentment and anger," Melinda said. "The anger that I had was far greater than the issues that I was angry at."

Jock and Melinda tried marital counseling, but Melinda found it easier to ignore the cause of her pain than to face the demons of her past. Melinda convinced herself that the problem was her marriage partner. She severed ties with Jock and moved on, but being single again felt odd. Eventually Melinda and Rick discovered that they were both newly divorced, and they reconnected.

Their friendship soon grew into a romance. Yet even while dating, they would fight about Rick's preoccupation with Cole. Rick believed Melinda's insecurities would disappear once they were married. After they tied the knot, Rick discovered he couldn't have been more wrong.

The daily war had begun.

✿ ✿ ✿

Sunday mornings were tense in their household. Naturally Melinda wanted to raise Billy in the church. Rick had agreed to tag along if Melinda and the baby went to his preferred church over at the beach. He was comfortable there. But Rick made it clear: attending did not equal believing. Melinda disapproved of his attitude, saying, "If the pew catches on fire while you're sitting there, I'm moving."

As nurses, both parents worked long hospital shifts all week and took care of Cole and Billy during the weekend. By Sunday morning, they were stressed. It was hard getting everyone dressed, pressed, and polished for church. One Sunday when Melinda was frustrated, she started shouting insults at Rick in the front yard. Another time, Melinda raked her nails across Rick's face. When friends asked about the raised red marks, Rick pretended he had scratched himself on a bush while doing yard work.

"She was just so angry, she hated my guts," Rick recalled.

Rick wondered what he had done to deserve this. Perhaps Melinda was his punishment for leaving Kim. If God existed, then He seemed intent on making Rick's second marriage a living hell. Despite that, Rick did not want to be the one to instigate divorce this time around. He would not play that part with his second wife. His escape would have to come another way.

Many nights Rick lay in bed, praying that God — or fate — would let him die. Suicidal fantasies thrashed against the shore of his imagination like wild, dark waves. He'd make it look an accident. He'd get outrageously drunk and smash his motorcycle headlong into a tree.

No! What was he thinking? His sons needed him to be their dad. Melinda must be mentally ill like her abusive father. If Rick could just hold on, she would implode. "I thought eventually Melinda would kill herself," he said. "She seemed so unhappy. She hated me so much. I thought that was what would get me out of this."

Most days, Rick tiptoed around Melinda, hoping not to provoke her. When she did explode, he remained calm. That upset her too.

"Why do you want to stay married? Or even want me here?" she'd yell.

"I don't know, Melinda," Rick would answer quietly. "I just kind of think…maybe tomorrow will be different."

Melinda would glare. "Tomorrow will never, never be different."

She wouldn't admit it, but Melinda was exhausted from the fighting. As happened in her first marriage, she decided that her husband was the root of the problem. One night after the baby was asleep, Melinda was sitting on her bed. Rick was standing nearby in the room and Melinda slouched there, thinking. "I told him I wanted to get out of the marriage," she said. "I can't live this way anymore."

Rick studied her. She expected to hear that same old speech about tomorrow being better. Rick surprised her. "If you really feel that way, Melinda," he said, pausing, "then maybe… you should go."

There. It was decided. This roller coaster was finally over. Melinda took a few days to figure out a strategy for the separation. She decided Rick should move out and let her stay in the house with Billy.

He refused, stating: "I will never leave you, Melinda."

Very well then! Melinda could not live with that man any longer. She announced that she would pack her bags and take Billy with her. Rick did not want her to take their son away. Impulsively, Rick uttered the only words that could have stopped Melinda from parachuting out of their crashing relationship. Even Rick was surprised to hear himself uttering the thought.

"You know, Melinda," he said, "if this marriage could be saved, I could almost believe that there was a God."

Can that old skeptic really be saying this now?

As an evangelical, Melinda had been trained all of her life to share the good news about the love of Jesus Christ with each and every soul who would listen. She would feel like the ultimate failure as a Christian if she abandoned her own husband at the first signs of a potential faith. But how could she stay married to Rick? Even the sound of his breathing annoyed her. He represented every irksome thing about her life.

Did God really think Rick would ever come to faith?

Melinda could not believe the choice that faced her; she silently prayed in protest: "God, you're playing dirty; I can't do this."

She felt like the Lord said, "Melinda, this is about so much more than a marriage."

Melinda yearned to walk out on Rick; instead God wanted her to walk out her faith in front of him. "I was trapped," she said.

She decided to stay, not knowing what to expect or if she could survive.

❀ ❀ ❀

Some weeks later, Rick went on his annual visit back to see his family in West Virginia. He took Cole and Billy. What a windfall! Melinda had an entire weekend to herself. She was emotionally worn out from working, fighting, and raising two young boys. Besides that, Melinda was constantly bickering at work with another nurse who acted like the boss of everyone. That uppity attitude did not sit well with Melinda.

At last she had some free time; yet she didn't have enough

energy to take a jog, work in the yard, or go to the mall. She needed to think, to unwind her emotions. She sat alone in the living room, peering into her inner self. The sheer weight of her anger overwhelmed Melinda. Collapsing, she turned onto her stomach and landed in a crumpled heap. She could no longer carry this load. Melinda poured her confusion and pain out to God. She dumped all of her messy emotions at His feet until she felt purged. Something stirred in her depths, an inner voice that refused to be silenced; Melinda felt God suggesting that she should befriend her haughty co-worker.

Befriend her? Melinda thought. *That woman is intentionally difficult!*

"Forget about all of that," God said. "Just follow me."

God was not interested in her excuses. He expected her to extend forgiveness to the annoying nurse. Melinda agreed that she would, but things with God were just getting started. Next the Holy Spirit prompted Melinda to acknowledge her hateful treatment of her husband. Melinda started to justify her behavior.

"Be kind to him," God spoke into her mind.

In the next instant, Melinda glimpsed herself through God's eyes: she felt completely selfish and broken. She was a wastrel, a black hole of hatred who had tormented both of her husbands. Melinda felt a strong internal nudge. She could still change, but this was her final chance. If she refused to soften, then...she felt a ravenous spirit of darkness and despair pressing in on her. It was as if her very soul was in jeopardy, a fate that her own legacy of hatred had created. She was staring into the abyss.

"Save me Lord," she cried.

Sobs wracked her chest. Rasping, Melinda rolled over onto her side, propping herself up on one elbow to catch her breath. Warm, blurry tears ran down her cheeks; the taste of salt spilled into her open mouth. When the tears finally dried and her ribcage stopped shaking, Melinda collapsed onto her back and lay still on the carpet. She couldn't get up; she couldn't speak. She was helpless; she was empty. In that vacuum, she had a vision.

Melinda saw herself as a blue marlin, fighting and fighting against being reeled in. God was on the other end of the line, trying to draw her close. "I never left you," God said. "I have always been there. The one who walked away, it was you. It was always you."

"Lord, I do see," Melinda said, choking out the words. She had been conditioned from an early age to come up swinging in order to survive. Now she was so tired. She had fought her father, she had fought Jock, her first husband, and she had fought Rick. Without knowing it, she had even fought God. She'd spent years feeling defensive, feeling angry. Using a mental picture, Melinda hoisted herself over the side of the boat and lay there, helpless, on the wet and slippery fiberglass surface. "I surrender," she said. "I am flopping my big self into the boat. I'm done. I have nothing left."

An enormous sense of relief flooded over her. The dark, threatening presence in the room had been vaporized. The pulsing peace of God radiated through her. "I felt that His strength was in me," she said, "but first I had to be brought to the end of myself."

Several days later when Rick pulled his pick-up truck into the driveway, Melinda came over and enfolded her husband in a giant hug. Her genuine affection startled Rick.

"Melinda was a different person," Rick said. "She said, 'I don't know if you can ever forgive me, but please let me try and make it up to you.' It was like I went away and when I came back, Melinda wanted to be my friend."

❁ ❁ ❁

It wasn't easy. Much like physical therapy hurts while it heals, her transformation would prove long and painful. Melinda worked at being kinder because she wanted to obey God. But she battled against rage, weighed down by a lifetime of baggage. "I could still poke his eyes out with hot pokers," she said. "I could get so self-absorbed with my own bitterness."

Now that Melinda was marching to orders from a Higher Power, she had to ignore her explosive feelings and offer tender acts: a pat on the hand or a gentle reply. "She said, 'I don't love you, but God said if I stay with you, I will love you. I just have to be obedient to that,'" Rick recalled.

Rick's dismissal of Jesus still rankled Melinda on a daily basis. Some neighbors organized a group for dessert and Christian fellowship. Under pressure from Melinda, Rick went along once but afterwards he refused to return. "I'm not sitting around a room singing "Kum Bah Ya" and telling people my troubles," he said.

Melinda was a born-again Christian living in the Bible Belt; frankly, her husband's unbelief embarrassed her. And God expected her to be kind to him? The next two years were the hardest of her life as she fought against her own ugly inclinations. "I have never known the Lord like I did then," Melinda says. "He was always with me. He walked me through the darkest of nights."

She was an emotional wreck: she cried at church. She cried at home. Her sense of insufficiency overwhelmed her. Melinda begged God to keep her tucked under His wing, to keep her close enough that she could smell Him.

"I was so helpless, so defensive, so raw," she remembered. "In those days, I did not move without God."

One day she felt God prompt her to buy her husband a Bible — and to get his name embossed on the cover. What? She even had to personalize the Bible?

"That will be another $20, Lord," she whined. She went to the bookstore and ordered a NIV Study Bible, resenting every penny of the $78. One night at a Mexican restaurant, she handed Rick the new Bible, its pretty blue cover trimmed with silver edges. "Here, God told me to get this for you," she said in a flat voice. She was not a cheerful giver.

Yet Rick was honored by the gift, especially by the addition of his name. "I've never had anything like this," he said. She shrugged. Thank the Lord, not me, she suggested flippantly.

Once Rick had his own Bible, he actually started reading it.

Melinda felt she should preach to him about Jesus, to persuade him of his need for the Savior. "God said, 'You've done quite enough talking. You work on yourself. I will take care of Rick,'" she recalled. "He said the last thing Rick needed to hear was the sweetness and kindness of Jesus coming from this wicked mouth."

Melinda silenced her tongue on the many evenings when Rick would nest in his overstuffed blue armchair and read that Bible. Melinda wondered if any seed was taking root, but Rick kept his musings to himself. Once while Melinda was watching Rick, God suggested she tell her husband that she loved him.

But she did not feel love for him. Wouldn't that be a lie?

Not if she had faith that God could supply the emotions. *All right Lord,* she thought, *but he had better not say anything back.*

Taking a deep breath, she rushed past Rick, lightly patted him, and squeaked, "I love you." She scampered away. This felt risky. She was acting sweet and making overtures to a husband whom she still didn't like. When she needed strength the most, Melinda felt an almost physical presence of the Lord.

"I would wake up in the night and know He was there," she said. "He would let me know. I felt grace over me at all times." She felt bathed in warmth, in a comforting peace inside her body. She felt that sense of well-being, of all things being right with the world, in a way she had never known.

"He would speak to me, not audibly, but in other ways," she recalled. "I spent a lot of time in the Word. He would lead me to scriptures to bring me comfort and confidence. He made me begin to have a softened heart."

Melinda felt supported in her efforts by her neighborhood Christian group. Rick had refused to go for several years, and Melinda had given up trying. "One night when I was going, Rick said, 'Can I go with you?'" Melinda said. "I almost fell over on the floor. This time, it was not anger, it was happiness."

Amazingly, her husband started attending the group weekly. Rick came to admire the other men: one was a former Air Force pilot who would shed tears over his love for Jesus. Another guy had been the captain of his baseball team at The Citadel, a local military college. Rick had never known men like these, paragons of masculinity who were devout believers. Rick liked his neighbors, but he was still tallying the score on Jesus. When one of their wives asked Rick to pray aloud for her prayer request during the group, he declined.

He had his limits. He could only be pushed so far.

Rick didn't hear it yet, but soon he would. God was calling his name.

One Sunday morning at their seaside church, Rick was kneeling beside Melinda during Holy Communion. He was muttering the standard confessional, reciting words he had repeated countless times: he had not loved God with his whole heart, he had not loved his neighbor as himself. Out of nowhere, Rick felt startled by the presence of the Holy Spirit rushing into him. He was suddenly alive with newfound faith and keenly aware of the existence of a spiritual world.

"It was like God smashed me in the face," he said. "At that point, I realized we weren't talking about the whole congregation; we weren't talking about the guy in the next pew. We were talking about me. I knew that day that my life would never be the same."

Rick was astounded at how quickly his faith grew and flourished. How did any of this happen? Rick pondered the unexpected move to Charleston, the ravage of the hurricane, the guilt of his divorce from Kim, the wrath of Melinda – each experience had directed him toward the pivotal moment in time when Rick was truly born again.

Melinda understood that her obedience to God had been the catalyst for Rick's conversion. God was true to His promise. Before long, Melinda fell in love with the new person that Rick had become.

✿ ✿ ✿

From then on, Rick hungered to know as much as possible about

God. He listened to the audio Bible every day while riding his exercise bike. Rick would also pray while he pedaled. A year later, unexpected thoughts started popping into his head about attending seminary. Rick didn't mention this to anyone. "It was just too weird," he said.

One day, Rick was talking to Melinda in the kitchen. They were planning their week. Melinda stopped talking mid-sentence and stared at him oddly. "You want to go to seminary, don't you?" she asked, sizing him up.

Rick was stunned. "Why do you say that?"

She smiled. The Lord had shown her something about seminary in a dream. At first, Melinda thought she was being called to the ministry. But the Lord had said, "No, not you, Melinda. It's Rick."

Melinda's premonition confirmed God's call for Rick. As unexpected as it seemed, apparently God had plans for him to join the clergy. The process would evolve slowly, but once the decision was finally made, Rick was surprised to be facing opposition. Well-meaning people didn't want him to throw away his career as a nurse anesthetist. His father thought someone had brainwashed him. His best friend at work thought he was wasting his intelligence, saying, "I am so disappointed in you."

Rick faced other worries. The seminary where he'd been accepted was several states away from Cole, now a teenager. Rick felt he was leaving his son when he needed him most. Rick was taking a huge risk for this. He could only trust that God knew what He was doing.

Rick would come to question that assumption frequently during the next three years. Life at seminary felt more like a breathless ascent of Mount Everest than a celebration at the summit. Other students seemed to thrive in the theological setting, but not Rick. His science skill set didn't match the academic requirements of writing lofty papers. And public speaking, are you kidding? He was the introvert who didn't want to expose himself by praying aloud, the guy who didn't like to speak to the minister after church. On a personal level, Rick was older than most of the students. Perhaps hardest of all, he endured an almost physical pain from missing Cole.

"I honestly thought I had not heard God correctly," Rick said. "For two to three years, I was probably clinically depressed. Yet Melinda would just encourage me. You can do this. It will be okay. Without Melinda there, I would have come home. I know I would have."

Melinda agrees. "It's like when you get in a dark place and you can't see the light," she said. "It was overwhelming to him."

Yet in a surprise twist, God had given Rick exactly what he needed: a wife who loved and nurtured him. Day after long day, buoyed by Melinda, Rick hung in there. After he finally graduated, Rick, Melinda, and Billy returned to Charleston to be near Cole again. Rick managed to continue his nursing career while working as a part-time priest. His faith, along with his earthy empathy, have touched countless people in both the hospital and church setting.

When a young wife in his parish lost her husband to suicide, Rick didn't pretend to have all the answers, but his humble concern and steady trust in God's love offered a soothing balm. When elderly members became too frail to go to church, Rick faithfully visited them, bringing Holy Communion to their bedsides and reassuring them that somebody remembered them.

Even from the pulpit, Rick's homespun sermons and personal stories allowed people to see how the God of the Bible was still at work among His people in the modern world. In his gentle way, Rick allowed people to catch a glimpse of God's compassion and patience.

No one ever saw this coming. "It is a true miracle of God," Melinda says. "Rick was the most unlikely man to have that happen."

"God equips people for what He calls them to do," Rick said. "He is just so powerful."

❀ ❀ ❀

For Group Discussion

1. How did Melinda feel about her husband? What was her initial reason for being angry?

2. What clues do we have about Melinda's childhood, and how was this impacting her attitude?

3. After having a baby, Melinda wanted to be a housewife. How did Melinda react when Rick told her that she needed to keep working? What was his reason?

4. Rick said, "I used to dread coming home to Melinda." Describe the atmosphere in their home. When have you experienced a similar home or work environment?

5. What role did religion play in hurting their relationship? Why were Sunday mornings so difficult? What was triggering all the stress?

6. Why did Rick cover up for his wife's behavior when she scratched his face?

7. Rick thought God might be punishing him via Melinda. Why did Rick feel he deserved to be punished? What promise did he make to himself in an effort to amend for his past?

8. How would you describe Rick's reaction to Melinda's constant verbal attacks? What wild thoughts ran through his mind on how to escape?

9. What kept Rick from doing something rash?

10. Eventually Melinda decided that she would move out and take the baby. What surprising thing did Rick say that rocked her world?

11. Why was this the last thing Melinda wanted to hear? What did she say to God about Rick's statement? What did God say to her?

12. When Rick went off for a weekend and Melinda finally had time to herself, what was the first thing that the Holy Spirit brought to Melinda's attention? Next the Lord spoke to Melinda about Rick; what was she told?

13. When she saw herself through God's eyes, what did Melinda see? How did she feel after her surrender to her Heavenly Father?

14. What did Melinda do as soon as Rick returned from his trip? Was it easy for Melinda to change? How did God meet her at her place of need? What does this tell you about God's character?

15. Why was it hard for Melinda to buy Rick the Bible? How did he respond to this gift? What might have happened if Melinda had refused to follow God's voice?

16. When Melinda was tempted to preach to Rick, what did the Holy Spirit say to her? Does this surprise you?

17. How did the Lord begin to soften Melinda's heart? How did Melinda's obedience lay the foundation for Rick's conversion?

18. Did God keep His promise to change Melinda's feelings for her husband?

19. What astonishing plans did God have for Rick? How was Melinda a pivotal part of this?

20. In thinking back over the entire story, what was the turning point for Melinda? For Rick?

Reflection

"Beloved, if God so loved us, we also ought to love one another."
1 John 4:11

"No one can come to me unless the Father who sent me draws them."
John 6:44

God is a god of processes. In creation, things change gradually and sequentially. How did God walk Melinda through her transformation with patience? Did He ever ask her to do more than she was ready to handle? Likewise, reflect on how the Lord gently but steadily drew Rick into faith. In what ways is He calling you to transform? What barriers of resistance might you need to break down in order to obey?

Room for Your Thoughts & Observations

CHAPTER *FOUR*/Lessons in Violence

"If you talk back, I am going to hurt you."

Danielle & Darius married on Mar. 25, 2000

D arius sat there, one hand resting on his forehead, with his eyes closed, reflecting. Relentless scenes of drama from his teenage years marched through his mind, tormenting him. Most of his life, Darius had mimicked his father's pattern of anger and violence. Like his dad, Darius had used outbursts to get his way, especially with the girl he loved. In the final days of high school, Darius had nearly lost his true love and future wife over a black eye. How could Danielle have stayed with him through all their frenzied fights?

"I tore her hair, or I would grab her arm," Darius recalled. "She'd grab my arm. It was just abusive. But after all the pain, we still loved each other."

Much of the time, things were good. Their names had been on everyone's lips at their school in Moreno Valley, CA.: 'the Two Ds', Danielle and Darius — a long-haired, glamorous Filipino girl with a flashy sense of fashion coupled with an athletic cool cat with a million-dollar smile. Darius's upbeat, charismatic personality brought out Danielle's playful side. Deep in her soul, Danielle sensed that they belonged together, even when her parents disapproved of her dating a black boy, even when her friends worried about Darius's temper and her safety.

"It's just a love that you cannot explain, when your heart is alive and awakened," Danielle says. "From the first day that we started out, I just felt so much love for him."

A robust attraction cinched them together with an invisible

tether. Yet when they clashed, neither desired to give in first, at times leading to a volatile war of wills.

✿ ✿ ✿

It was around Halloween of their junior year. The Two Ds and another couple had tromped through a local Haunted House, laughing and screaming their heads off at the ridiculous vampires and cheesy ghouls. But the fun ended on the ride home.

Darius's best friend Cedric was driving, his date snuggled up next to him. Danielle and Darius were sitting close together in the backseat when abruptly, something went wrong. Danielle started mouthing off at her man. Darius hated feeling like she was smarter than he was. He pushed her flat against the back seat, pinning her down with the weight of his outstretched body. "You @#$!!," he screamed. "You talk too much. You always have something to say. Why don't you just shut the #&*@!! up. You never listen!"

Danielle pushed back, biting Darius's arm and shouting up into his face. No man was going to dominate her. As the scuffle intensified, Cedric's date urged him to pull over and park. They needed to break up the fight before someone got hurt. But Cedric shook his head and kept right on driving.

"That's just Darius and Danielle," he stated.

Reared with abuse, Darius could ignite quickly. "If my mother got out of line verbally, my dad would grab her," Darius said. "He thought the only way to really control her was to be violent…I was conditioned to seeing that. If you talk back, I am going to hurt you."

In fact, the shameful legacy of uncontrolled anger had grown for several generations in Darius's family tree. As a girl in Detroit, his mother Charlene had suffered abuse at the hands of her father until her parents had divorced. Sadly, when she was grown, she married a man with a destructive temper and returned to her role as victim. In that way, Charlene passed the bitterness of paternal abuse onto her children. With this background, why should Darius be any different?

"I thought it was a genetic thing, but it's not true," Darius says now. "A lot of it is just your believing you are violent as opposed to your believing: I am a man of God."

Looking back, Darius credits God for sending vital help during a desperate childhood. "If you saw my life today, you would never know that I come from this past," Darius says. "I don't know why God spared me, but I feel blessed that His hand is on me."

❀ ❀ ❀

Her very first time, Charlene had gotten pregnant. She was 16, and her boyfriend, known as Rocky, was 17. They didn't marry, but they stayed together after Darius was born in 1975. Darius spent his first 10 years in the Inglewood section of Los Angeles, a neighborhood left to impoverished ethnic groups. His parents drank heavily and spent their limited money on crack cocaine. The same crazy stuff went down with most of the adults he knew.

"Everyone was high," he said. "My parents were addicted to crack cocaine all throughout my childhood." In contrast to the drugs, his mom loved Jesus and could toss a Bible verse at him to suit any occasion. "But knowing God's word and living it are two different things," he says.

Darius was about five years old when his parents decided to get married; it was the happiest day of his life. The wedding took place on his maternal grandmother's large front lawn – Grammy lived in a tidy bungalow a few blocks away. This is the same strong woman who, years earlier, had left her belligerent husband. Fleeing Michigan, Grammy had escaped with Charlene and her three other children to California and established a safer and healthier life. As family matriarch, Grammy kept a watchful eye over her clan.

Charlene and Rocky's wedding was a milestone for the family. Young Darius marched down the grassy aisle in a tan suit and white dress shirt as the ring bearer. He felt so proud.

"We rode from the wedding to the reception in my Uncle Reggie's candy apple red convertible," Darius recalls. "The day was amazing. Everyone danced, partied, and drank all night." The little ring bearer drank from a glittering champagne fountain; as the bubbles tickled his nose, Darius was afloat with the sensation that his future would be happier.

However, the joy wouldn't last: without steady jobs, his parents often struggled to hold things together. Sometimes they'd lose their apartment for falling behind on the rent; other times, landlords evicted them after receiving incessant complaints about the noisy fights. "When my father was drinking, he was either really friendly or really angry," Darius recalled.

One night when Darius was in third grade, things got heated. His dad was a former golden gloves boxer; for occasional fun, father and son would lace up the gloves and spar. But this time his dad was agitated from drinking liquor. He announced that they were going to box barehanded. "We were just goofing around," Darius said. "He's moving, and I'm moving. He went to duck his head, and I hit him on top of his head. I wasn't trying to hurt him, but it must have been harder than he was prepared for, because he started hitting me with his fists and taking his belt off."

The nine-year-old boy fell to the floor and crouched. "Dad!" Darius called out. "I'm sorry! I didn't mean it. It was an accident."

His mother stepped into the room; Darius begged her to rescue him. "I'm sorry, there's nothing I can do," she said. "You shouldn't have hit him." She turned her face away, biting her clinched fist. Charlene knew too well what Darius would suffer. Maybe the beating would teach her son to be more careful.

For now, the punishment must be endured. Though Darius pleaded for mercy, the thick leather belt whipped his back through his thin cotton T-shirt and lashed against his exposed arms. After several anguishing minutes of repeated blows, his dad paused. Large puffy welts appeared across Darius's forearms. His throat felt clogged with the thickness of tears; Darius gasped for breath. "At that point, I think it must have dawned on him that, 'I should probably stop,'" Darius recalled.

Seeing his father's hesitation, Darius scrambled away in ragged retreat. "I go to my room," he said. "I hate him. I want him to die and I'm praying, God, kill him, take his life. I hate him."

The next day, bruised and tender, Darius gingerly apologized. "He said, 'I'm sorry too, but you shouldn't have hit me like that,'" Darius recalled. Without a defender, Darius had to live with the uncertainty of his father's moods. "There were no older men that I could really run to and say my dad is doing this and that," Darius said. His two uncles were his playmates, a mere year or two older. Even so, his mom's extended family network did provide a temporary safety net. Whenever Darius's parents were between places to stay, they could crash on a couch or sleep on a pile of blankets at a relative's home.

They managed to hang on for several years — until things got worse.

By the time Darius was about 10 years old, he and his parents were staying in a series of dirty flophouses; home to roaches and strung-out people, the rooms had water stains on the ceilings, burns on the ragged carpet, and dingy cold-water showers. Without a kitchen, his mother cooked on a hot plate, and meals were haphazard at best. "I was in the fourth grade and I was barely going to school," he said. "My mom and dad were high, and my dad was selling drugs."

Darius was afraid; his life was plunging into chaos. He did the only thing within his power: he called his maternal grandmother, confessing the ugly details of his daily existence. Recently Grammy had remarried and moved to a cheerful new subdivision about an hour away in Moreno Valley. Before long, Grammy had swooped in and whisked her grandson out of Inglewood. Darius could stay with her, his two young uncles, and her new husband.

"She saved my life," Darius says. "She took care of me and is the reason I am here today."

✿ ✿ ✿

In the new neighborhood, aptly named Sunnymeade, every cozy house smelled of fresh paint. It was unbelievably quiet and amazingly crime free. Kids passed footballs back and forth in the street or scrambled behind bushes while playing Hide and Seek in the neatly landscaped yards.

Grammy and her family were the only black people on the block, but their white, Asian, and Hispanic neighbors mixed easily with them. Darius, a cute, talkative kid who had never met a stranger, soon had plenty of friends. While he missed his mom, Darius adored his new home. Grammy made sure he and his two uncles, now living like brothers, were washed, clothed, and well fed.

"It was the happiest I'd been in a long time," he said. He went to school. He gained a healthy amount of weight. He felt safe. Grammy's new husband had converted their garage into a little preschool, and it was thriving.

Two years later, when Darius was in the sixth grade, his mom gave birth to another baby boy. She and the baby left Inglewood and moved to Sunnymeade to stay with them. She had missed her big boy, Darius; also, Charlene said she was worn out from fighting with Rocky. "I'm done," she told them. "I am through with him."

Darius was thrilled to have his mom back. She went to work in the family daycare business. After several months, Darius's mom could finally afford her own apartment. When Rocky found out about her success, he wanted to join them. "He would sweet talk her and B.S. her, saying things like, 'I'm not high, I'm not drinking. I miss my family. I'm sorry,'" Darius recalled.

For some time, his mom resisted. Charlene didn't need Rocky; she was dating new boyfriend, a Latino named Roy. Darius didn't like seeing his mom acting mushy with some random guy. Once, Darius walked into the apartment and caught his own mother having sex with this creep. Humiliated, Darius slipped away to his room before either of them realized he was there.

Days passed, yet Darius couldn't erase the image of their entwined bodies. The next time his dad called, Darius blurted out about seeing his mom with Roy. Rocky realized he needed to win back his wife before it was too late. He got Charlene on the phone and cried about how much he missed her. Next he poured on the charm, proclaiming that he had straightened up for good. Given the chance, he would be a model husband and father.

He was persuasive. "She wanted to believe all of that," Darius said. When his dad moved into their apartment, Darius was hopeful. "I was glad that he was going to be back, and that Roy wasn't going to be there," he said. "No matter what, as a kid, you want your family to be together."

But Rocky never got a job and, before long, he was openly drinking again. The allure was infectious, and soon his mom had ventured back into the party scene. By now, Charlene was more responsible; she limited herself to episodic binges. During the week, she earned a living at the daycare, keeping her younger son with her while she worked. On the weekends, she and Rocky would party.

It wasn't all bad. His parents were sociable types with natural rhythm, and they knew how to create a festive atmosphere. On Saturdays, Charlene and Rocky often pushed back the furniture, invited friends over, and danced the night away. The happy music of the Isley Brothers, Marvin Gaye, and Luther Vandross filled their den. Darius liked watching them groove, especially when they partnered for the Cha-Cha. His parents taught him to do the sexy Cuban dance; this hot-blooded skill would help to break the ice with Danielle in the ninth grade. Her strict parents had never danced the Cha-Cha-Cha around their living room.

❁ ❁ ❁

Danielle was the third daughter born to Filipino parents within three years. After several moves, her family had settled in Moreno Valley. Her father worked as a Chief Petty Officer in the United States

Navy; he would be gone for months, shipping out to Europe, Asia, and other far-flung places. Danielle missed her Daddy when he was away.

"I was the last daughter to be born, and of course his hope was for me to be a boy," she said. When that didn't happen, he improvised. When Danielle was small, he called her 'Boy' and cut her hair into a bowl cut. As she grew into elementary school, they'd shoot hoops in the driveway and watch his beloved L.A. Lakers on TV. When she was in middle school, he painstakingly taught her to plant and dig in his large fruit and vegetable garden. "I felt very close to my father," she recalls.

Her mother filled the role of disciplinarian. A full-time nurse, she was detail-oriented, a hard-working perfectionist. Often, she came home exhausted from a 10-hour workday to a household with three girls, an absent husband, and her own parents, who lived with them. When frustrated, Danielle's mom had a short fuse. "We lived in fear of her," Danielle said. "I understood discipline...I understood what would happen if we crossed the line with my mother."

Her mom pushed her girls to excel. They attended Catholic church and Sunday school regularly; they endured being browbeaten by her tirades as she urged them to become doctors or lawyers. Fearing mom's displeasure, they made sure to get good grades. The girls also performed major chores around the house: vacuuming dust balls from behind the sofa, cleaning streaks off windows and patio doors, mopping grease off the kitchen linoleum. "She was very specific about how we were to clean," Danielle recalled.

They appeared as a model Filipino family, but in the darkest corners of their spotless home, unnatural things went on that even Danielle's mother didn't see: the girls' maternal grandfather was molesting them. He had abused Danielle from her earliest childhood years.

"He would lure us with candy," she recalled "He would take us back into the bedroom and lock the door. He would have a pornographic magazine in there, and he would start touching me." The grandfather forced a variety of sexual acts upon the girls. Her parents and grandmother had no inkling. "We were scared to tell," she said. "He told us if you ever tell anyone, you are going to die."

For several years, each girl thought she was the only victim. When the sisters discovered their shared secret of shame, they began to commiserate. Eventually, when the two older sisters were in middle school and Danielle was in fifth grade, the girls felt strong enough to stand together against their grandfather's traps. The abuse ended, but the trauma had hardened Danielle.

"It made me feel that even the people who love you the most are going to hurt you," she says. "I lived my whole life with a guard around my heart. I wouldn't let anyone all the way in. I was totally protecting myself."

Danielle was mentally strong; she managed to compartmentalize the pain and carry on as a normal teen. She was interested in boys, she liked fashion, and she spent time working on her appearance. She and Darius started out as friends in middle school, but by the ninth grade, things had heated up between them.

✿ ✿ ✿

Danielle always pushed the envelope on style. She was petite, only five feet tall, with wavy brown hair hanging down to the middle of her back. "I was known as the girl who always hooked up her hair," she said.

Danielle wore many styles: ponytails or braids, half-up, half-down dos, or curly waves hanging loose. At times, she teased it into a big Texas hairdo, perhaps coloring it pink or electric blue, then anchoring it with enough aerosol spray to coat it stiff. Danielle knew how to finish her look with put-together outfits.

The effect, along with her beautiful legs, caught Darius's eye. Two decades later, he still remembers what she was wearing the night their friendship sparked into a romance: a black-and-white polka dot skirt topped by a matching form-fitting zipper jacket. It was the school's homecoming dance in the gym; nervous ninth-graders,

Danielle and Darius hung out in the bleachers with a mutual guy friend and one of Danielle's sisters.

The deejay played songs from Smokey Robinson, New Edition, and other 1980s pop bands. Their group chatted and watched kids bump and twist on the basketball court.

Unexpectedly, Darius asked Danielle to dance. They'd been friendly for several years, but nothing more.

"I wasn't really attracted to him," she recalled. "He was kind of cute, but he wasn't really my style." Darius was a short, mahogany-skinned boy, skinny and not much taller than Danielle. He was wearing gray acid-washed jeans, black Creepers (loafers with a platform), and a black T-shirt. His toothy smile was bright, even in the dimly lit gym. Suddenly feeling a bit shy, Danielle hesitated, but then agreed to give it a go.

On the dance floor, Darius asked if she knew how to Cha-Cha. Danielle shook her head. No one else was Cha-Chaing, but Darius went to work, playfully teaching her the swaying moves. Danielle loosened up and started enjoying herself. Under his confident guidance, she felt safe letting down her guard.

"In that moment, it didn't matter what other people were doing; they just kind of disappeared, and it was like it was just us," Danielle said. They stayed together, dancing and laughing for the rest of the evening, and a switch flipped. "It was very strange," Danielle recalled, "there was this weird energy that I felt; we both mutually felt an attraction that was alarming."

When a slow dance played, "we were holding each other so close you'd think we'd known each other our whole lives," Darius recalled. In the days following the dance, they started sitting together in the lunchroom and chatting by the lockers. Their mutual friend, Ron, encouraged them to date. Darius liked Danielle, but he considered himself a ladies man, and he wasn't ready to give himself a yellow card from the playing field.

"He was very, very flirtatious with everyone," Danielle recalled. "His personality was very sociable, very charming. Everybody loved him." Darius often joked about his dad being a pimp because of his numerous friendships with sexy women. Darius had the same swagger.

"At that point, he had lots of little girls he was trying to entertain," Danielle said.

But Darius had a deeper side, and in private notes and letters, he revealed hints of this to Danielle. They would write back and forth, sharing feelings and thoughts, steadily growing closer. Danielle was an honor roll student while Darius preferred sports and social life. "He and his friends used to cheat off my history paper in Miss Horrigan's class because they knew I would get an A," Danielle said.

A model student, she also played on the school tennis team. One day Darius walked her to practice after school. Between the gym and the tennis courts, they found themselves momentarily alone. "We have this good chemistry," Darius said. "We're laughing about something and then, we just end up kissing." Their lips met but after a few moments, Danielle broke away.

"Wait a second," she said. Nimbly she pulled a wad of bubble gum out of her mouth. Darius laughed and pulled her back close; their mouths parted, and they shared a long, lingering French kiss. The intensity surprised them both. "It was the best kiss I ever had, oh my goodness, yes," Darius recalled.

"He didn't know I could kiss like that," she said, giggling.

Afterwards, Danielle wondered: were they dating now? "I wanted to be with him," she said, "but Darius had a player mentality and wasn't so sure about settling down and having a girlfriend."

The issue soon came to a head. Darius decided to make a move for Danielle's pretty friend Pamela. One day Darius puffed out his chest and presented Pamela with a teddy bear he'd won at a local carnival. Pamela reluctantly accepted the gift, then she showed the bear to Danielle. Danielle felt like she'd been hit in the gut. How insulting! Her crush was flirting with her BBF.

"I remember feeling like what? Why would he do that?" Danielle said. "I thought we had a connection."

Darius soon realized he'd been a fool. Pamela wasn't interested, and now Danielle refused to speak to him. Yet Danielle's hurt feelings served a purpose: Darius understood how much Danielle actually cared for him. He was touched; they made up and started officially dating.

Soon everyone in school knew them as the inseparable Two Ds.

✿ ✿ ✿

By their sophomore year, they were having sex. Danielle felt fiercely jealous of any perceived rival for her man. At times, the physical intensity of their relationship morphed into a fracas. "We were the Reality TV couple of our high school," Danielle says. "People were like, 'Did you see Darius and Danielle fighting by the lockers? He pulled her hair. Oh, and he just hit a girl.'"

They had been quarreling when a female student stepped between them, trying to protect Danielle. The girl ignored Darius's command for her to step aside, so he slugged her. He was the one in control here, and he wouldn't put up with anyone interfering — not even Danielle. If she tried to storm off during an argument, he would seize her. "I'd grab her arms, and it'd end up with me restraining her," he said.

Time and again, concerned friends urged Danielle to break up. "Why would you put yourself in a situation where you will continue to get hurt?" they asked. No one understood her dogged commitment. "I loved him," she said. "I was able to see his heart and know that was not what he wanted to do. It always ended up in violence because that was what he was modeled, that is what he was taught."

Another problem plagued their relationship: Danielle's parents. Mr. and Mrs. Balino thought Darius was merely a friend to their daughter, but even that level of racial mixing made them uncomfortable. Darius recalled when he and other students gathered at Danielle's house before a Key Club trip to a local theme park. She lived near the school, so the kids congregated there to arrange rides. "Me and my boy Cedric, we had to wait outside the house until the other

15 – 20 people came out to get in the cars," he said. "I could never go in Danielle's door."

The sweethearts had some allies: Danielle's older sisters adored Darius, and they helped keep the relationship hidden. All three sisters felt their parents were too strict, especially when it came to curfews and boyfriends. No matter how much Danielle might beg, her parents would never approve of Darius. "Color was really hard for them to see beyond," Danielle's older sister Edie said. "I think the heart of their disapproval of the relationship was worrying about their daughter. They associated her being with Darius as an indication that she was going wayward."

That image was reinforced one day when Mr. Balino came home unexpectedly for lunch. Lightning was about to strike: Danielle, Darius, and one of his buddies were already there, having snuck away from school during their lunch break. The Two Ds had slipped upstairs while Freddie, a lumbering, 6-4 black guy, had happily padded into the kitchen to chow down. "He opened the fridge and was making himself a six- course meal," Darius recalled.

Bam! The back door slammed. Danielle broke away from her boyfriend's embrace and listened. Someone was yelling at Freddie.

"That's my dad!" Danielle said, panicked.

She couldn't make out the words, but her father's voice sounded boiling mad.

She had to rescue Freddie and distract her dad so that Darius could sneak out. Danielle scrambled back into her clothes and raced down the stairs, taking two at a time. Her abrupt entrance into the kitchen caused her dad to turn his head, giving Freddie an opportunity to escape. Big Freddie jerked open the back door, jogged across the grass, and heaved himself over the fence. A clean getaway.

Danielle's father shook his fist and called after the disappearing figure of the teenage boy. When he turned again to his daughter, Mr. Balino's eyes flashed with ire. What had Danielle been doing while the Incredible Hulk was helping himself to all the cheese and luncheon meats in the household?

Fixing her makeup? she suggested.

Her Dad didn't buy it. He pushed past her to investigate.

"Daddy, please. Wait!" But he didn't stop.

Even before hearing the heavy footfalls on the stairs, Darius had scooted into the adjoining bathroom. His hands were shaking so much he had trouble putting on his clothes. He lay against the cold tile floor and managed to wriggle into his jeans just as the bathroom door flew open. Danielle's dad towered over him.

"What the hell are you doing here?" Mr. Balino yelled. "Why are you in my house? Get the hell out of my house!"

"Yes sir!"

Darius crawled past his accuser, then scrambled to his feet; he bolted down the stairs, crossed the entry hall and tumbled out the front door. When he ran into his buddy at the street corner, Freddie burst out laughing.

"He thinks we got away," Darius said. "But then we could hear her dad yelling at the top of his lungs at Danielle. I asked my friend, 'Should I go back and help Danielle? Should I help Danielle?'"

They decided the sight of Darius would only add fuel to the fire. Instead, the boys ran back to school and found one of Danielle's sisters, quickly filling her in on the crisis. "You don't have to worry about my dad," Edie said, "but my mom is probably going to kill her."

Darius felt helpless. "Danielle's mom beat the hell out of her," he said. "They threatened to send her away. They said she had to choose, it's either me or them." From then on, Danielle told her parents the relationship was over; she created a convincing show of contrition, and Mr. and Mrs. Balino breathed a sigh of relief.

"But she'd sneak me into the house when her parents were upstairs," Darius recalls. "We'd do crazy stuff like that. We were young and in love, like Romeo and Juliet."

Luckily, the young lovers were not star-crossed everywhere. Danielle was always welcome at Darius's house. "I really loved Darius's parents," Danielle said. "I really saw the good in them despite the fact that they were strung out on drugs, abused alcohol, and had anger in that way. They accepted me right away as their daughter and just loved me."

Most of the time, his mom seemed normal; she didn't party during the day and, if she did drugs, it was always behind closed doors. Of course, Jesus was always part of the package with Darius's mom. She took Danielle to church with their family and often shared Bible verses with her.

Danielle went to the services, but she wasn't buying into the concept. She disliked her childhood experience in the Catholic tradition, resenting the use of guilt and the many tedious rituals, and by high school she had dismissed religion as an empty shell. In hindsight, she credits Darius's mom with preparing the soil of her soul. "She was definitely the one who was planting the seeds and praying over us," Danielle said.

❁ ❁ ❁

Those tiny seeds would wait more than five years to sprout; in the meantime, Danielle and Darius entered their senior year. That October, each was named to the Homecoming Court.

Naturally, Danielle dreamed of waving at an adoring crowd, a rhinestone tiara setting off her long, curled locks, and a bouquet of red roses cradled in her olive-skinned arms. Her favorite guy would serve as her escort, looking handsome and sophisticated in his formal wear: a tuxedo with a white jacket and black lapel.

Surely their peers would vote for them as king and queen; after all, the Two Ds were a package deal. On the school's basketball court, Darius played point guard, so Danielle managed the team and kept score. On campus, if Darius and his friends were relaxing at the outside lunch tables on the quad, Danielle would be there, cuddling knee-to-knee beside him. They were voted cutest senior couple and had their picture taken for the annual – she leaning against his chest as he flashed a Cheshire-cat grin.

"That has kind of been the theme for who we are as a couple," Danielle says. "We always did everything together, always."

Then Homecoming hit. The ceremony started at half time with the glamorous members of the Homecoming Court riding around the football field in convertibles. The guys drove while the girls perched on the backs of the open cars to show off their full-length gowns. The tension mounted as the members of the court processed to the center of 50-yard line. Soon everyone would know the winners!

"The crowd was going crazy," Darius recalled.

Each nominee had received a sealed box; the chosen king and queen would find a star inside; everyone else's boxes would be empty. Danielle held her breath while they all lifted the lids in tandem. Who would claim the royal status?

A star! Darius shouted with joy at being named Homecoming King. He looked at Danielle expectantly.

But it was Ambrosia, a new black girl with striking good looks, who was whooping and waving. As King Darius and Queen Ambrosia stepped forward to greet their cheering fans, the beaming queen clutched the king's arm.

Danielle choked back tears. *Don't cry, not here in front of the whole school,* she told herself. The last thing she needed was black mascara trailing down her miserable face. As soon as possible, Danielle fled the stadium for home.

The Homecoming King wanted to see her after the game, but Danielle snubbed him. "She was pissed," Darius said. "I didn't understand it. If she had won and I didn't, I would have been happy for her. Why should I be mad at you for winning?"

"It was just a hard thing to swallow at the time," Danielle said. "I was mad at him, even though he had nothing to do with it." They soon made up, but the pain from her public humiliation lingered in the form of Ambrosia.

"For the rest of the year, Danielle and Ambrosia were never cool after that," Darius said.

On Graduation Day, this female tension would flare up again, triggering a fight that would almost end the entire love story. Darius didn't realize how much distrust was brewing in Danielle's imagination. In the meantime, he ran into fresh trouble at home.

✿ ✿ ✿

The day started like any other school morning; Darius was preparing to head out for class. "My mom said something to me about getting ready to go, about having my homework, and I answered her in an annoyed voice," Darius recalled. "I was like yeah, mom, I already did it; I've got it."

His father was lounging around the bedroom. Hearing his son's flippant tone, Rocky strode out to confront him. "Don't you ever talk to your mother like that," he growled, getting in Darius's face.

"I didn't mean anything," Darius sassed back.

"Who do you think you're talking to?"

Before Darius could respond, his dad grabbed a 10' metal candlestick from a nearby table and swung it into his son's chest. The blow struck him hard; Darius struggled to breathe.

By now, Darius was big enough to match his father in a fight; but Rocky was quick and didn't give him the chance. "Next he takes the candleholder and hits me across the head with it," Darius said. "I tried to swing back at him, and he hit me in the head again."

Cedric was living with them at the time. He heard the commotion, ran into the room, and broke up the fight. Escorted to safety by his buddy, Darius stormed out.

"I go to school that day and I say, I am never going home," Darius recalled. Before class, his friends often gathered at the outdoor lunch tables near the quad. Danielle wept when she saw his bruises. It was a Friday. Darius told Grammy he was staying at her place. That night, he and Danielle went out to a party with one of his teenaged uncles. People were drinking 40-ounce Mickey's malt liquor, and for the first time, Darius over indulged.

"I wanted to get drunk," he said. "I had never felt like that before. I think I thought it might numb me from the pain."

Despite his initial impulse to move out, Darius calmed down

over the weekend, so he returned home Sunday night. When his dad saw him, it was as if nothing had even happened: no apologies, no show of concern for his injury. "I knew then that as soon as graduation came, I'm leaving here," Darius said.

The remaining months of school sped by and, before they knew it, Graduation Day had finally arrived. The morning broke sunny and fresh in that winsome California way, with no hint of the terrible drama to come.

As a special favor, Darius was allowed to drive his father's Honda Excel to the graduation practice at 9 a.m. The students rehearsed on the school's grassy quad. Afterwards, a bunch of the seniors were meeting at a diner for a big breakfast. Darius and Danielle, chatting with friends, were among the last to reach the student parking lot. Suddenly, a girl's lilting voice floated up from behind them: "Hey there, Darius."

Relaxed and happy, Darius put his hand in the air and playfully waved. Then he turned to see who had hailed him: Ambrosia was grinning in a flirtatious way, right in front of Danielle. "Ambrosia was being mischievous," he said.

Jealousy raced through Danielle at the sight of Ambrosia's beckoning smile. "Why did you say hi to her?" she demanded. Her mind leapt to wild conclusions: *something must be going on between my man and that harlot.* "Did you fuck her?"

No! Darius tried to explain — nothing like that had ever happened. Danielle was too upset to listen. She started to run away, but Darius grabbed her, keeping her from fleeing. Danielle's suspicions had hijacked her brain. She couldn't stand for him to touch her. She writhed, trying to break free.

"Let me go home," she yelled. "I don't want to talk to you!"

"Danielle, listen to me, it's nothing," he shot back. "Just get in the car and let's go."

Danielle struggled, trying to get Darius's hands off her arm. But Darius opened the passenger door and forced her into the Honda's front seat. She sat there, wondering whether she should trust him as

Darius jumped into the driver's seat. He suggested they skip breakfast and go to his house where they could talk things over privately. The pleading in his voice felt manipulative. Danielle didn't believe a word he was saying, and she felt trapped. She tried to hop out, but Darius held her back. Danielle started kicking wildly. Her foot smashed against the glass.

"Don't kick my dad's window," Darius shouted.

"Let me out of here," Danielle screamed, pounding her fists on the dashboard. They pushed and pulled against one another in frustration. In the fracas, his fist struck her upper cheek. The blow was hard; she knew immediately that she would have a bruise. In all their previous scuffles, Darius had never struck her like that.

"You hit me!" Danielle cried out. "You punched me in the eye! How could you?"

Darius was frightened and confused. He let her go; Danielle threw open the car door, lurched out and sprinted toward her subdivision. Darius sat there for a few beats, trying to collect himself. A minute later, a friend showed up in the parking lot. "I just saw Danielle running and crying," he said. "What did you do to her?"

"I honestly don't know what happened," Darius said, still in shock. He drove toward Danielle's house, hoping to talk to her. She was running down the street, crying. When she saw him, she changed directions and ran across a neighbor's lawn. He decided to go home and give Danielle some space to calm down. He told his mom about the fight.

"Darius, did you hit that girl?" she asked.

"No, I wasn't mad at her," he said. "I was trying to grab her, and I felt my fingers poke her in the eye."

Danielle went home and looked in the mirror; sure enough, a purplish bruise shone around her right eye. "How can I go to graduation like this?" she asked her reflection.

With the help of her best friend, Danielle found a large pair of designer sunglasses that covered the unsightly swelling and discoloration. She was furious at Darius.

I deserve to be treated better than this. "He had never left any marks on me that anyone would be able to see," she said. "This was an obvious crossing of a line. You damaged my face, you made it public, and I can't do this anymore."

Before long, the news of the fight was all over school.

Darius didn't know it yet, but he was Public Enemy No. 1. Next to his wedding or his 21st birthday, graduation was supposed to be the biggest day of his life. He'd even purchased a new Rayon suit for the occasion: a two-toned black and royal blue number with a black shirt and matching tie. Yet that afternoon during the ceremony, everyone – even the teachers — shunned Darius. He tried explaining to Danielle's sisters, but even they refused to listen.

That night the entire class celebrated with a trip to Disneyland, and Danielle wore her sunglasses in the dark. Instead of being the life of the party, Darius shuffled around the theme park without a friend. "I had to go to graduation night by myself," he recalled. "It was the worst night of my life. This is the last night of our high school experience, and we should be together enjoying it and instead, I am alone."

After the park closed, charter busses returned the graduates to school. Darius used a pay phone to call his parents, then he waited for his ride. "Out of nowhere, here comes Danielle walking through the quad with her sunglasses on," he said. She refused to acknowledge him. He stood there, helpless, watching as she walked home alone in the dark.

A few days later, Danielle left for college in San Diego without even saying good-bye.

✿ ✿ ✿

Danielle's older sisters had moved to San Diego; the eldest, Edie, had always been like a second mother to her, and Danielle planned to stay with her for a month until she could move into her dorm at San Diego State. Luckily, Danielle was still living there when she discovered she was pregnant. "But I had made the decision not to be with Darius," Danielle recalled. "I kept it from him. I didn't want him getting involved."

Danielle wrestled with her options before deciding to have an abortion. She dreaded everything about the process. "I was scared," she said.

Ending the pregnancy didn't seem like a morally defensible thing to do — after all, she had grown up Catholic. She had been taught the value of unborn life. But religious doctrine seemed less relevant than the fact that she was on the cusp of expanding her education, her opportunities, and her future. In just a few weeks, Danielle was supposed to ease into campus life as part of a summer program for incoming minority students. Being pregnant would interrupt her forward momentum, perhaps temporarily, perhaps for good.

Danielle had the abortion. "It was so selfish. Looking back, if I had known God, there is no way I would have done that," she says now.

Darius was clueless about Danielle's trauma; he kept calling her at Edie's place in hopes of making up. His former sweetheart refused to come to the phone. "She wanted nothing to do with me, not even a conversation," Darius recalled.

Darius wrote Edie a letter, sharing his side of the story about the black eye. "Edie called crying and said she forgave me," Darius said. While the big sister kept Danielle's abortion secret, she offered Darius a sympathetic ear, advising him to allow Danielle some distance and some time. When she was ready, Danielle would talk to him.

Darius couldn't leave it at that. In desperation, he turned to a Higher Power. His mother had raised him on Biblical promises and church services. Religion had never mattered much to Darius, and it would still take years before faith transformed his daily life. Yet Darius wondered: would God help him fix things with Danielle? When Darius prayed, he felt like he had received an answer: don't give up.

Darius continued to reach out, writing emotional letters and sending lengthy apologies on cassette tapes. Nothing worked. "She was done with me," he said. About a month after graduation, Darius was living at home without a job or any plans for the future.

"I felt like I was either going to go to jail or die," he recalls. "Everyone I knew was running the streets, getting in trouble."

His lucky break came, unexpectedly, from Danielle's sisters. After Danielle had moved into her dorm, Edie suggested that Darius and his buddy Spike move to San Diego. They could crash at her apartment for a few days until lining up their own place. Edie recognized that Darius and Spike were both good guys from challenging backgrounds who needed a helping hand.

They joined Edie in La Jolla, an affluent part of town near the college campus. Everyone in her apartment complex was a student, and before long Darius and Spike had moved down the hall to room with one of Edie's male friends. The other sister, Doris, found Darius and Spike jobs at the cinema where she worked; neither had a car, but the theater was directly across the street from their apartment. "Things just fell into place – it was just kind of magical," Edie recalled.

The move changed everything. Suddenly, Darius had hope for his future. "Edie showed me a life that I had never lived before," Darius said. People here weren't running the streets – they were motivated students working toward professional careers.

"I think that (improved) environment inspired him to do the right thing," Edie says, "to get a job and not go for what his friends back home had done, easy money." Working in a cinema wasn't glamorous, but it was an honest living, and Darius felt good about himself.

Through her sisters, Danielle kept track of Darius's progress; eventually she allowed him to talk to her again. That went well, so they started hanging out as friends. "I wasn't putting pressure on her to get back together," he said. "Everyone was having their own space. But she could see me grow and change and work hard...

"The more time we spent together," Darius says, "the closer we got." Before long, Danielle realized that her passionate feelings had never died. It was impossible to resist Darius. "We both felt this draw to each other," she said.

They reunited, but an old conflict remained lurking the background: the disapproval of Mr. and Mrs. Balino. "If my parents had known she was with him, they wouldn't have sent her to college or helped her buy a car," sister Edie says.

Danielle and her sisters were careful never to mention Darius to their parents. Physical distance worked in their favor, and the secret was safe for now. The Two Ds were back full force, sharing as much time together as possible. After class or work, they enjoyed partying with friends, getting drunk, and smoking weed.

"We would work, stay up partying until two, then be up by six in the morning to go to work again," Darius said. "I was living a life that was not connected to God at that time."

Since leaving home, Darius had lost interest in his mother's Baptist church. Through new friends, he found himself drawn toward the Nation of Islam; he was excited about studying the Koran and applying its teachings in a black-power way. Darius had attended junior college, and he now saw the Christian faith as a legacy the slave masters had forced on his people. He questioned all his childhood assumptions about the church.

"I'm searching at this time," he said. "I always knew there was a God, but I want to know if I am going to believe in this God, it is because that was what I have decided and not because that was what my mom and dad had told me I was going to do."

Eventually, his inquisitiveness about Islam fizzled out, in part because he had withdrawn from the junior college to work full-time as a manager at a GAP store. He lost contact with the Islamic circles and focused on making friends and enjoying life. Darius floated free from any organized religion until a buddy from work started raving about a popular youth pastor, a former defensive back for the San Diego Chargers. This guy was amazing, his friend kept saying. You've got to hear him to believe it.

Curiosity tickled Darius whenever his friend started talking about the preacher, Miles McPherson. For some reason, Darius wanted to see this pastor for himself. Danielle had a car, and she agreed to drive them to a service. Horizon Church had a lively atmosphere, with Christian rock music and lots of 20-year-olds who were pumped up about their faith. Pastor Miles was hip and funny, light-skinned and ruggedly handsome, with a compelling testimony. He was open about his past as a former NFL player and crack cocaine user who had surprised everyone by morphing into a Jesus freak.

"For the first time in my life, someone had articulated the Gospel in a way that I could understand," Darius said. "In my heart, it is really resonating with me at this moment."

He and Danielle continued to go and hear Pastor Miles from time to time. One night following a worship service, Darius felt an unusual hunger to pray. After Danielle dropped him off at his apartment, Darius retreated into his bedroom and shut the door. He fell to his knees on the wall-to-wall carpeting. He closed his eyes, clenched his hands, and prayed the most honest prayer he could manage. "Jesus, if you are real, I want to experience you," he whispered. "I want to have one of those moments when I know it is you."

Several years would pass before this prayer would be answered. At the same time, Danielle was also rethinking her concept of God.

"As a Filipino, you are born Roman Catholic," she said. "It was very ritualistic for us. We did the Catholic thing, but faith-wise and spiritually, we didn't know the Lord. It was more just making the actions." She'd heard Bible stories growing up, but they had never seemed relevant — until Pastor Miles.

"Every message I heard from him was speaking directly to me," she said. "It felt like God was personally delivering it to me." During altar calls, she wavered. She wanted to go down, but something kept holding her back.

"We are still not fully committing," Darius said. "We are not saying okay Lord, we're all in. It's more like me praying but not really doing all the right things toward it."

Whether or not they realized it, they were inching toward God with baby steps.

❁ ❁ ❁

Eventually, Darius and Danielle started living together. "When her parents would come to visit, I would leave," he said. "I would have to hide my stuff and disappear. After a while, I finally said I can't do this anymore. You need to make a choice. I can't continue to hide." So Danielle wrote a letter and revealed that she had reunited with her high school boyfriend. The worst happened. "They disowned her," Darius said.

At this point, Danielle was working as a couture specialist at Saks Fifth Avenue in downtown San Diego. Darius was working in sales for Coca-Cola, calling at convenience stores and liquor stores and submitting their orders; he was making $35,000 a year. "That was a lot for us back then," Darius said.

They had been attending church regularly for several years when Danielle became pregnant. They agreed they would not bring the baby into the world without being married. "We always knew we would get married," she said. "This just sped up the process."

The new life growing within her made Danielle yearn to be closer to her Creator. "My spirit was being reborn, and I was pregnant," Danielle says.

She grew in her trust of God. The little girl who had been betrayed by her grandfather, who had feared letting people get too close, was maturing into a woman of faith. She began to see that God offers pure love and, despite the trials and troubles in her life, He could be trusted. "There is a bigger plan for us all," she decided.

While still pregnant, Danielle went to work in sales for Tony Robbins, a popular self-help guru and motivational speaker. She worked hard and soon received a promotion. Her life was on the upswing. Danielle and Darius planned to wed in Las Vegas when she was about seven months along. "I wasn't the bride I had always imagined being when I was a child," she jokes. "I was pregnant, and I had braces."

Darius's family would meet them in Las Vegas for the ceremony, as well as Danielle's sisters. When Danielle invited her parents to attend, she steeled herself for another rejection. Yet her mom surprised them, agreeing to join the celebration at the glitzy Vegas hotel. This would be her first grandchild. "Danielle's mom decided she wanted to be part of the baby's life," Darius said.

Her father was still holding a grudge for the way Darius had behaved with his beloved daughter back in high school, and he refused to attend. But his heart would not always be so hard. Almost a year later, when Danielle's uncle died unexpectedly, her extended family gathered for the funeral in northern California. She, Darius, and eight-month-old Bryson made the six-hour trip.

At a gathering after the services, Darius was surrounded by his wife's large Filipino family. "I was the only brother there," Darius says, laughing. Everyone felt the elephant in the room.

One of the cousins complimented Mr. Balino on his handsome new grandson. "He was a beautiful brown baby with lots of curls," Darius says. "He was a happy baby."

Danielle tried to hand the baby to her father, but her dad refused to take him. Yet sister Edie noticed something soften in his face. "I could tell my dad was kind of interested in him, he was kind of watching him," she said.

Later in the afternoon, the men in the family congregated on the patio to drink beer, trade stories, and get away from the women. Darius, feeling a bit awkward, was standing around trying to act like one of the guys, even though no one had offered him anything to drink. Danielle's dad scrutinized his son-in-law for several seconds while the other men looked on. Then Mr. Balino spoke the first words he had directed at Darius since catching him on the bathroom floor.

"Darius," he said, nodding toward the cooler. "Get a beer." The thaw would be long and slow, but it had begun.

❊ ❊ ❊

At home, Darius wasn't adapting to his new roles. "I hadn't adjusted yet to being married, I didn't know what it meant to be married," he said. "We had been together for years and years, so to me it was just doing the same things."

Darius was faithful to his wife, but he didn't alter his cool cat lifestyle. He would head out to watch the game with his buddies, then roll into a bar, hanging out until the wee hours. In his mind, it was the wife's job to change diapers or wake up for the 2 a.m. feedings. He remained the same sociable guy, talkative and hot-tempered, quick to flash, but also quick to win points with his musical laugh. Somehow he always wound up being the center of attention. He and Danielle still fought more than they liked; it was automatic for him to insult her when angry, or to use his physical strength to intimidate and control her.

Neither one knew how to break the pattern.

But the focus of their lives was about to shift: Danielle continued to perform well in her sales job, earning the chance for them to attend a Tony Robbins motivational workshop over a long weekend. "It teaches you a lot about yourself," Darius said. "They ask good questions, things you wouldn't ask yourself."

Through the psychology and self-discovery sessions, Darius realized something: "There were a lot of things I was holding onto." The new insights were cracking open the door to the process of extensive change. More would follow.

That same year, their beloved Pastor Miles founded his own church, The Rock Church in San Diego. More than 3,000 people turned up for the first service, including Darius and Danielle. The powerful praise and worship services would eventually attract up to 16,000 members. In their usual synchronicity, Darius and Danielle dove headlong into hand waving, nondenominational Christianity, each accepting Christ. Danielle and Darius trusted the promise of scripture that they were new creations. Yet the old habits lingered.

Things shifted after 2001, when Danielle attended *A Date with Destiny*, a longer workshop with Tony Robbins where she learned to write a personal mission statement and lay claim to a higher purpose. Although Tony's teachings are psychological and secular, his program complimented what she was learning at church. "It worked hand-in- hand," Danielle said. "You do need skills sets and specific strategies for helping you through your day-to-day life and your mindset."

When Danielle returned home, Darius noticed her peaceful demeanor. "I don't know what they did to you in those six days, but I want that glow," he told her. Danielle felt as if a change had happened on a cellular level. "He said even my smile was different," she said.

During the soul searching, she discovered that she had suppressed and diminished herself by worrying too much about what others might think. She vowed to be her true self, in the purest form, without fear, whether that meant literally dancing for joy, sharing her penchant for silly accents and impersonations, or being bold enough to pray aloud and offer spiritual encouragement and counsel to others. "Since that moment, I haven't looked back," she says. "That's who I've been since that experience."

✿ ✿ ✿

A year later, Danielle's continued success in sales allowed her to send Darius to the same *Destiny* program; there, God would finally answer his prayer about having an unmistakable Jesus moment. "The whole week, I cried like a baby," Darius recalls. "I knew God had set aside this time for me to have this experience."

He was one of about 5,000 people in the grand ballroom at the Westin Hotel in Palm Springs, CA. During the assemblies, the participants closed their eyes and listened to music while Tony led them through a series of contemplative questions. In those reflective moments, "I would really feel the presence of God in my soul," Darius said. The initial teaching focused on discovering your core values and deep motivations: who are you going to be? Why are you going to change your story? What are the consequences of your old story? Darius decided his old story went like this: "I am just like my dad. My dad didn't love me. I am going to end up hurting my wife just like my dad hurt my mom."

At last Darius realized he had been reading from a dismal life script: his father's anger and violence had trapped him. Despite wanting a happy family, Darius had mimicked his role model and inflicted pain on his wife. The conference sessions, coupled with deeply personal mental exercises, presented Darius with a shocking truth: he had the power to make creative choices. The insight struck him like a body blow; without grasping it, he had been choosing to let frustration lead to verbal and physical aggression.

He found himself facing his moment of destiny: "I could decide whether or not to hit my woman, to be aggressive, or just walk away." With every cell in his body, Darius suddenly believed that he could change, and now he hungered for the opportunity. He felt the transformation was almost more than he deserved.

"I hadn't been living my life as I should," he said.

He was humbled by thinking about the people who had offered help during his darkest moments. First, God had sent Grammy to take him into her home in Sunnymeade. Later, He sent Danielle's sisters to provide a fresh start in San Diego. More recently, He sent Pastor Miles to explain the Gospel in a way that Darius could digest. Without all of this, Darius knew that he might have become a drug addict; he might have ended up in prison; he might have died on the streets. Instead, he had a good job, he was married to a beautiful, loving woman, and together they had a healthy and handsome young son.

Darius finally had his moment where he felt the undeniable love and presence of God and Christ. God had always been at work in his life, protecting him, calling him, but somehow Darius had missed seeing it.

He felt sorrow over his own resistance, false bravado, and stubbornness. Now Darius wanted nothing more than to crawl into his Heavenly Father's arms and lie there in safety and love. In his heart, he surrendered everything to God, including the pain and confusion of his past.

A new desire was awakened in his soul: "I wanted to be a man of God. I wanted to be a man who takes care of his family physically," Darius said. "I had to communicate this with Danielle. I had hurt her physically and emotionally so many times. Finally, now I understood who I wanted to be."

❁ ❁ ❁

Darius longed to share his awakening with the person he loved most in the world, but he could not see Danielle until the end of the conference. During the last day, the workshops focused on finding and maintaining an ideal love relationship. In the closing assembly, Tony was on stage, encouraging the audience to reflect on what they had learned about themselves during the week. He looked out over the packed ballroom and asked who wanted to share his or her story. Hundreds of extended hands waved in the air, vying for Tony's attention.

"Out of nowhere, I raised my hand," Darius said.

"You, over there," Tony said.

Tony was pointing at him! A runner dashed over and gave Darius a microphone. Video cameras with bright lights pivoted in his direction, capturing his testimony on film. Danielle had come for the closing ceremony, but Darius could not see her in the packed ballroom. It felt as if the entire world were watching. Would he be able to express himself and convey to his wife how much he had changed?

As soon as Darius opened his mouth, heartfelt words came gushing out.

"I realize that I already have the ideal relationship," he said. "My wife and I have been together since ninth grade, believe it or not. I caused her so much pain, physically and mentally, early in our relationship because I didn't love myself. She, instead of being defensive, loved me more."

Darius pledged his constant love for Danielle. He thanked her for giving him a son. Then he made her a promise: "Danielle, there's not a day that God allows me to breathe that I won't spend loving you, worshipping you, and appreciating you, because I love you so much." The crowd erupted into cheers and thundering applause.

"Where's Danielle?" Tony asked.

She was seated in the back of the ballroom, holding her breath. "It felt like a movie moment, when everyone disappeared," she said, "and it was the first time he'd ever said those words to me. I knew it was genuine." She sprang up from her seat, rushed down the aisle to Darius, and threw her arms around him. They embraced, tears flooding their faces, barely aware of the whistles and cheers surrounding them.

The victory program ended after 9 p.m., and Darius and Danielle tried to slip out quickly: they needed to drive several hours to pick up their toddler from relatives who were babysitting. But it was hard to break away. Darius was swamped by admirers.

"I couldn't leave," he recalls. "There was a line of people wanting to shake my hand and tell me how my story had changed their life...it was overwhelming."

Even in the parking lot, he heard, "Darius!" People were screaming his name, waving, and giving him the thumbs up. The rush of attention made him feel fully alive and completely in touch with his higher self. He had changed. He was a new man. And everyone around him recognized it.

Suddenly, Darius felt the total acceptance and love of Jesus Christ flood into his heart. It felt as if all the good will and affirmation of the crowd were directing the divine love toward Darius. For the second time that week, he remembered his earlier prayer for such a moment. Darius felt that his small life mattered, and he was in awe. God had been faithful, but could he? Would his motivation survive after he had returned to the real world?

The following week, friends at work listened to his dramatic redemption story with interest, then suggested that his good intentions might soon fade away. How could Darius live as a peaceful man amidst the tensions and tussles of daily life? But he wasn't the only one with fresh skill sets, visions, and goals. Danielle had also learned specific strategies and methods of self-motivation. She and Darius would hold each other accountable.

"Our relationship since that time has just been extraordinary," Darius says.

"We're different people," Danielle says. With the support of their church home, they started spending time with other Christian couples. That fellowship has helped keep them on track. "This is something bigger than us," Darius said. "It's all God. He kept us together for a reason."

They make a solid team, now hosting a small Bible study group for couples in their home. She organizes behind the scenes, and Darius takes the stage and leads. "People meet him, and it is instant love – his warmth, his compassion, his charisma," she says.

Darius also volunteers as head football coach for their son's team; not surprisingly, Danielle primes and oils the football machine as the team mom. They also create and act in short, funny videos about married life that they post on YouTube. "They are really devoted to each other and their family," sister Edie says.

After suffering through a series of miscarriages, Danielle finally had a second child, Baje, now a preschooler. "For years and years, I have been praying for another baby," Darius says. "Then God gave us this son. Now I am involved in everything. I am so in love with this baby."

Danielle's father stays with them during the week to care for his youngest grandson. That in-law relationship softened several years after Darius had his watershed moment. They had invited Danielle's father to one of the Tony Robbins retreats; there, Darius found himself awkwardly paired up with Mr. Balino for a one-on-one exercise. "The last person I wanted as my partner was Danielle's dad," he admits. But the Lord led Darius to embrace the opportunity; he heard himself saying words he never imagined he could say.

Darius looked straight at his father-in-law. "Mr. Balino, I want to apologize to you for disrespecting your house in connection to your daughter in the 11th grade," he stated. "You have done an amazing job raising your daughters. I just hope I can be half the dad that you are. I'm so sorry, and I just apologize." They embraced, and both started crying. "That was the moment that our relationship changed," Darius says.

Darius has experienced mending in the relationship with his parents as well. Over time, as his father aged, his temper mellowed, and the abuse tapered off. But deep-rooted doubts remained for Darius about whether his father had ever loved, valued, or respected him. After much introspection and prayer, Darius understood that his father did love him, in spite of the anger.

"It took a lot of self-discovery to get to that point," he says. "God revealed it to me." Through faith, Darius has managed to let go of his painful past. Instead of being bitter, he practices gratitude. "God has shown me that my identity comes through Him and not through my dad. He is my father," Darius says. That epiphany has freed Darius to be a loving, supportive father to his sons. "Those two boys, they live a completely different life because of Him," he says.

As in any family, the parents sometimes disagree, but Danielle says they have new ways to reconcile now. "We'll look at each other and make each other laugh," she says. "Or we'll forgive and let go of it. Anger doesn't exist when you know Jesus and the gift of forgiveness."

God has orchestrated all of the healing, Darius says.

"It's definitely not because of me," he said. "I did everything I could to ruin it. It breaks my heart to think about it. I can't believe I was that guy...I thank God for loving me enough to forgive me and to allow Danielle to forgive me."

Danielle still can't get enough of Darius. Each day, she loves him more. They take frequent trips together and spend weekends enjoying outdoor activities with their children; they each post affectionate pictures on Facebook in which she is sitting in his lap or he is posing with her cheek-to-cheek, relaxing at the beach, enjoying a football game, sharing a meal among friends at convivial gatherings.

"We're absolutely best friends," she says. "I don't think either of us can imagine our lives without the other."

In spite of everything they have weathered, Danielle knows she is in the arms of the right man. "When people say I've found my soul mate, I think it goes even deeper than that," Danielle says. "God has selected this man for me, and he is my appointed mate."

❀ ❀ ❀

For Group Discussion

1. How would you describe the relationship between Darius and Danielle during their high school dating? What kept them together?

2. What was the reaction of Darius's friend when things got tense in the car? What did Darius think about his tendency toward abusive behavior?

3. What did friends say to Danielle about her boyfriend? Why did she ignore their advice? What did Danielle's parents think about Darius?

4. What prompted the big fight during graduation weekend? How did things get out of control?

5. Why did Danielle feel everything had changed?

6. After moving to San Diego, how did Darius gradually win her back?

7. What attracted Darius to the Nation of Islam? How did this alter his view of Christianity? Why did he eventually drift away from Islam?

8. How did Darius and Danielle respond to Pastor Miles? What did he offer that appealed them? How was he offering something different?

9. While alone in his room, what was Darius's secret prayer?

10. How did Danielle's pregnancy change their relationship? How did it change Danielle's outlook?

11. How did Darius's growing faith influence his response to the information presented during the Robbins conference? What clarity did Darius receive about his power to make meaningful choices?

12. In what way did Darius suddenly see evidence of God in his life?

How was his prayer answered to have a special God experience?

13. What did Darius realize that he wanted to be?

14. How did their relationship change? As time went on, what helped them stay true to their new ideals?

15. How does 2 Corinthians 5:17 apply? "For if anyone is in Christ, he is a new creation; the old is gone and the new is here." How is Jesus Christ able to shape a broken human being into a new creation?

16. Why do good intentions so often fail? What does it take to make lasting change?

17. In thinking back over the entire story, what was the turning point for Danielle? For Darius?

Reflection

"I can do all things through Christ who strengthens me."
Phil. 4:13

"Do not conform to the pattern of this world, but be transformed by the renewing of your mind. Then you will be able to test and approve what God's will is--His good, pleasing, and perfect will."
Romans 12:2

Consider the areas where you may be conforming to negative patterns which others have modeled for you. Ask God to grant insight into where and how He wants you to change. Ask the Holy Spirit to guide you as your write down your thoughts. Read over your own words to see where you need to begin. Pray for God to lead you forward, step by step. To receive, you must believe.

Room for Your Thoughts & Observations

CHAPTER *FIVE* / In Sickness and Health

"I threw daily temper tantrums with God."

Beth & David married April 9, 1983

After only five weeks of dating, David shocked Beth by asking the most serious of questions. Would she consider praying during the next 30 days to see whether God wanted them to marry? As a Marine, he was being reassigned soon, and he needed to know.

Although the suddenness of the idea surprised her, at age 24, Beth could imagine marrying David, 22. Feeling flattered and hopeful, Beth solemnly committed to seek divine guidance during the next month. In tandem, David promised to pray fervently and listen for God's leading. Four weeks later, David and Beth both agreed: God was calling them to serve Him as man and wife. Eager to be united, they set a date to marry six months later. "When I met David, I had a deep sense that my path was with him," Beth said. "It sounds weird, doesn't it?"

The happy couple had discovered one another in a Baptist Singles Group in the Washington, D.C. area; each entered the relationship with an established conviction that God had a specific plan for his or her life. Those plans were seemingly meant to intertwine. In the exhilarating early stages of their romance, Beth and David had no forewarning of the physical and emotional pains which lay ahead.

How could they guess that, at times, David would be tempted to run away from a wife besieged by chronic illness? How could they guess that Beth's physical limitations would profoundly eclipse their future happiness? How could they guess that, at times, Beth would prefer divorce to living with David's anger and bitterness?

Yet with God's help and personal grit, David and Beth would paddle their way through swirling rapids and finally emerge safely into calmer waters. After more than 30 years of marriage, Beth and David now work together like a well-honed team, always searching for ways to serve others and their Creator.

"Over the years, we decided that life on this earth is boot camp for heaven," Beth said, "and whatever we do or face here is God's preparation for what He wants us to be in eternity."

✿ ✿ ✿

Beth started out lucky, born into a cheery, supportive home as the middle of three children. Her family had moved a bit in her early childhood, but by the time Beth was in sixth grade, they had settled into the close-knit village of Council Groves, Kansas, population 2,500. "It was a sheltered existence," Beth said. "This was the kind of place where we safely rode our bikes all over town."

Beth's parents had married young; as their family grew, they worked hard to provide for their son and two daughters, placing a priority on their education and development. "My parents really liked one another and had a strong desire to be good parents," Beth said. "I don't remember them ever missing a school play, ball game, or art show – my parents were always showing up."

Sunday was set apart as a family day: Beth and her siblings, led by their parents, attended the local Methodist church before gathering around the dining table and digging into classic American meals such as fried chicken, green beans, and mashed potatoes. "My parents had a rule that dinner time was a time to enjoy one another," Beth said. "Consequently, at the dinner table no one was allowed to fuss at anyone else. We told jokes and talked about our day, and we actively worked at enjoying one another."

Afterwards, the family might play a board game or go for a stroll, spending a leisurely Sunday afternoon together. Like her childhood, Beth's teenage years in Council Groves were happy. After high school, she enrolled at Brenau Women's College in Gainesville, Ga.

During college, Beth began to ponder the standard soul-searching questions: why she was here on this earth? Did she have a specific purpose? How did God fit into all of that? After much prayer, Bible reading, and introspection, Beth accepted Jesus Christ as the ultimate cosmic answer. At age 19, she became a born-again Christian. "There's a difference between growing up in the church and honest-to-goodness deciding to believe in Jesus Christ," Beth explained. "It was more of an evolution than a revolution for me."

At the same time, Beth had to focus on her immediate future. Graduation neared and Beth started looking for a job; one of her professors helped her land a staff position in the office of a United States Congressman from Georgia. At age 22, Beth graduated and moved to Washington, D.C. to work on Capitol Hill. She did not know a soul in the nation's capital.

"I liked living in the D.C. area as a single girl," Beth said. "There was a freedom and excitement. But it was also hard and sometimes, lonely."

Beth sought out friends with similar values and soon found a comfortable fit within a Young Singles Group at a large Baptist church in Northern Virginia; this wholesome crowd sat together on Sundays at the morning and evening worship services, went out to brunch, played softball in the park, or just spent time drinking coffee and socializing.

Beth dated a bit within the group before venturing into a serious relationship. She thought she might be falling in love. "To my surprise, about a year into our dating, the guy started dating another girl in the Singles Group and still wanted to date me as well," Beth said. "I was hurt and ended the relationship. After that, I decided that I had sworn off men...until David. What is that old saying, we make plans and God laughs?"

✿ ✿ ✿

In contrast, David had limped through a painful childhood in rural Jefferson County, Kentucky. David's mother suffered from severe depression and alcoholism. When David was in kindergarten, his mother was sent away for a two-month stay in a psychiatric hospital. Rounds of electric shock therapy didn't fix her; although she was able to return home, David's mother remained emotionally erratic and unreliable as a caregiver. As a child, David didn't understand what was wrong, but he knew the woman at the center of his world seemed fatigued and flustered. She wasn't happy or well put-together like the other moms in his small town.

Most parental duties shifted toward his dad, a local judge with a crowded court schedule. Still, the family managed to function with the help of David's two older sisters— until disaster struck again.

When David was nine years old, his father contracted a severe case of strep throat that permanently damaged his kidneys and rapidly diminished his health. David's sisters cooked meals and made sure their little brother got off to school, but by the time David was 13, both sisters had left home to pursue their own lives. His father was increasingly frail; his mother was unstable. David felt angry, abandoned, and afraid.

His stormy adolescent emotions must have worried his mom because she dragged him to church to see the Billy Graham movie "A Time to Run". Despite his reluctance to attend, David acquiesced and sat down quietly to watch the film with the rest of the crowd. Before long David felt Billy Graham's booming voice and direct talk of divine judgment stirring up feelings of alarm.

"The Holy Spirit touched me, and I had white knuckles on the pew," he recalled. David felt an urgency to respond and accepted Jesus Christ as his personal savior – right then, right there. He understood all too well, from watching his father's health sputter, that the human timeline was finite. "I thought if I am going to die, I do not want to go to Hell," he said.

This impulsive decision wasn't simply a defensive reaction that would fade shortly after the movie credits. David actually believed in something now, and he took his new spiritual commitment seriously, joining Young Life and other Bible study groups for teens. He wanted to conduct himself as a Christian, but he didn't yet have the maturity. Despite his best intentions, David still carried around a volatile mixture of testosterone, resentment, and frustration.

"Up to that point, I was not a model citizen," he recalled.

He could be rash. One Saturday afternoon, David and three friends vandalized a neighbor's home after the family had gone out for the day. "We threw mud balls on all sides of their house and also inside their house through the open windows," he said. "When confronted that evening by the man who owned the house, we denied the entire event and counter accused someone else we knew – and didn't like – in the neighborhood."

But another neighbor had seen the vandals, and eventually David and his friends were caught. He expected his parents to punish him severely. "Afterward, my father, knowing that we had lied to others and had lied to him and my mother — said nothing, did nothing, and made no mention ... it was literally radio silence," David said. He was shocked that his parents didn't have enough strength to correct him.

Ironically, their complete lack of authority scared David. He fell into deep reflection. Did he really deserve to get away with this? Did he want to wind up as a juvenile delinquent? He had made a commitment to God through Christ, and that meant he should be different.

"Around the same time that I became a believer, I started parenting myself," David said. "One parent was mentally ill, and the other one was terminally ill. Someone had to do something, and it had to be me."

David grounded himself for two months and steadily distanced himself from his rebellious friends. From then on, David held himself to a higher moral standard. During high school, it was David who stepped up to bear the brunt of his burdensome family life. For fun and fitness, David pushed himself as a distance runner on his school's state championship track team. Sadly, David was forced to give up his beloved sport during his senior season to drive his father, by now nearly blind from kidney failure, to thrice-weekly dialysis treatments. His father died when David was only 18.

Two months later, David shipped out to the University of Idaho on a Navy ROTC scholarship. "I realized I could either be a menace to society or a mentor to society," he said, then quipped: "I kind of split the difference and became a Marine."

He spent his summers in rigorous Marine training programs, jumping out of airplanes and taking leadership classes. Upon graduation from Idaho, David proudly received his commission into the United States Marine Corps. Determined to succeed, he reported to The Marine Officer's Basic School back in Quantico, located just 53 miles south of Washington, D.C., in Northern Virginia.

Before long, he had connected himself to the friendly Singles Group in Falls Church, VA., that would forever alter his trajectory.

❀ ❀ ❀

From the beginning, Beth noticed the fit young Marine. "In Sunday School, David impressed me with his knowledge of the Bible and his eagerness to apply the principles to his life," Beth recalled. She found herself admiring his self-confidence one afternoon when their Singles crowd went out to brunch.

Even with a Marine buzz cut, David couldn't hide the fact that he was losing his hair; one of the guys in their Singles group broke out a 'bald man' joke, lobbing it across the table at David. "Hey! That's okay," David volleyed back. "If the rest of you guys want to waste your hormones growing hair, go ahead." David ended the point in his favor with a cocky grin.

Beth was impressed by the way he handled the verbal rally. *This guy is really secure with himself,* she thought; *he is really comfortable with who he is.*

She didn't know it, but this intriguing Marine was about to become the love of Beth's life. They connected one Sunday afternoon because David didn't have any place to go between brunch and the

113

5 p.m. worship service.

Quantico was a bit too far for David to conveniently return to base between lunch and the evening service. Most Sundays, David hung out with a friend who lived closer to the church. One day David's buddy wasn't around at brunch, and someone pointedly asked David where he was going in the interlude. David shrugged. Maybe he would just go back to the church to wait. He had some things he could study.

Beth expected one of the guys to invite David over, yet no one did. "I had no real plans," she said. She was going back to her apartment to do laundry and clean; Beth told David that he was welcome to come along and study there.

He jumped at her offer. "We had a really pleasant time," she said.

Soon afterwards, David asked her out. "I found out she had her own washer and dryer," he joked. In truth, in that one afternoon of relaxing and chatting, David immediately felt that they fit together. "We agreed on so much," he recalled.

It was the summer of 1982; on their first date, they went to see "ET" and grabbed some dinner afterwards. They followed this up by seeing "Rambo" and a series of other movies. At first, they palled around and flirted within the larger context of the Singles set, but before long, they were dating exclusively. Besides being physically attracted, David was impressed with Beth's independence in moving off to D.C. to follow a good job. "She wasn't a homebody; she had struck out on her own," he said. "She was no wallflower."

In fact, Beth was the most special girl he had ever met. Just when things were clicking along, David's assignment to train at Quantico was winding down; he was due to be shipped out soon. He decided to act before he lost his chance.

After only one month of serious dating, David invited Beth into the Community Room of his Marine barracks. It was an open day for visitors in this shared parlor space, so groups of Marines and their families were sitting on the sofas and chairs, laughing and chatting about their plans. Yet as far as David was concerned, Beth was the only other person in the room.

"He sat me down and said I want to marry you," Beth recalled. "I was floored, absolutely floored." David suggested that each should spend the next four weeks praying to see if God wanted to use them as a team. If yes, they should marry. If no, they should split up. They agreed to seek God's will. Before long, they were promised to one another in marriage.

Looking back, David admits it all happened quickly, "but in everything I did, I either went big or I went home." His father's early death had taught David not to waste time. Also, "we did not have a whole lot invested yet," David explained. "It seemed like it would be better to get a green light or a red light from God before we fell deeply in love."

As Christians, they had decided to follow the Bible's guidelines for dating. That meant nothing more than hugs and kisses until they were married. "People give away too much of themselves too cheaply," Beth says.

"You should save as much of yourself as you can for marriage," David says. "The Bible says to save everything."

Once they became engaged, David wondered: how he could afford a diamond ring? He didn't have any savings or family money to help. After his father's death six years earlier, his mother had survived on a shoestring budget. For several years, David had sent her about 30 percent of what he earned, including pay from odd jobs and Social Security survivor benefits. Upon hearing the good news, his mother seized the chance to help her son, giving David the diamond ring from her 25th wedding anniversary. With gratitude, David reset the stone for his bride-to-be.

❀ ❀ ❀

Almost immediately after the engagement, the Marines shipped David off to tank training at the U.S. Army Armor School in Fort Knox, Kentucky. They were separated for five long months. "It was unbearable to leave each other's presence, and there was absolutely nothing sexual going on between us, so it wasn't that," David recalled. "We agreed on so much and outlined our lives together in what is now, looking back on it, very rare, extensive, and minute detail."

Above all, they looked forward to being parents and raising a brood together; they each felt children were one of life's greatest blessings. While she waited on the wedding day, Beth dreamed of her rosy future as David's wife. In the interim, Beth had stayed in Washington to work on her job and arrange the wedding plans. They made a deal. She wouldn't pester her fiancé with questions about the big event and, in return, he would be happy with whatever she devised.

"We agreed when we got engaged not to stress over the details," Beth said. "We decided that whatever happened, our wedding would be great, and we would just enjoy it."

They didn't plan on the April showers. When the wedding day finally arrived, the heavens opened and let loose an enormous storm. Relentless rain poured down, all day and all night. Then there was another unwelcome surprise. "The wedding cake turned out to be the ugliest cake on the face of the planet – it looked like the Leaning Tower of Pisa," David said.

When some of the guests saw the malformed cake, they were worried that the bride would be upset. Surprisingly, Beth and David laughed about it. "We were taking bets on whether it would fall over," he said. David, proudly wearing his Marine officer's Dress Blues, including the navy tunic, white cap, and white gloves, pulled out his military sword to slice the cake. More like a brick wall, the baked confection did not give way on the first cut. "The cake stood in resistance to the sword," David said. "It even tasted bad too!"

After the wedding, the newlyweds took three weeks to drive across the country on a honeymoon trip. Now that he had a wife, David couldn't believe how many bags and boxes she brought with her. "Prior to marrying me, everything he owned fit in the back of a pickup truck," Beth said.

Besides her clothing, Beth brought along her feather pillow, her tea kettle, her hair dryer, her bedspread, and all her other belongings.

They were traveling to their first home – Twentynine Palms, a Marine Corps Air Ground Combat Center – in the arid and blistering desert of Southern California.

It was already baking hot in May when they moved into base housing. The flimsy apartment felt about as solid as a cardboard box. Beth was unable to put away her linens for months because the paint remained tacky on the closet shelves. "The place was dirt cheap, but you get what you pay for," David said.

A brand-new Second Lieutenant, David worked as a platoon commander of enlisted men operating diesel-fueled armored tanks, affectionately referred to as "fifty-six tons of fun". The Marines would roll out into the scorching sands for several weeks with no showers. "We came home pretty ripe," David said. Some of the wives hosed off their sand-encrusted husbands before permitting them to cross the threshold. David had been looking after himself since middle school. He didn't wait for his wife to take action, but slipped into the garage, peeled off his sweaty, grimy clothes and started up the washer. "He has never asked me to do his laundry," Beth said.

While he was off playing war games, Beth busied herself setting up their modest home and then found a part-time job. They were stuck in a remote locale and, on weekends, the Marine families had to scratch around for interesting activities.

"There was nothing to do – no movie theater, only an officers' club, a pool, a base exchange – mostly people would get together and host potluck suppers," she recalled. David organized a Bible study, and they made a core group of good friends. There was plenty of camaraderie on base. "We gave each other a lot of support," Beth said. "Someone would help out if your washing machine broke, or another guy would get under the hood of your car if your husband was out in the field."

Beth had not yet considered the potential angst of seeing her husband shipped off to war. That fall, they both felt the reverberations from the bombing of the Marine barracks in Beirut, Lebanon. Islamic terrorist groups using truck bombs and other explosives killed hundreds of American and French peacekeepers in October 1983. David's former roommate was injured but survived. Several of his other friends were killed. For the new bride, the carnage hit close to home.

"This was my first eye-opener of that real-life kind of stuff," Beth said. The more experienced Marine wives taught Beth their tricks for handling the loneliness and uncertainty when a husband was sent into conflict. Their coaching would pay off in the years ahead: David would be deployed five times during his military career.

From then on, David and Beth lived with an unseen current of anxiety swirling in the underground passages of their minds. As a Marine, David owed his unflinching allegiance to the Corps and was expected to be prepared to leave home on short notice. When and if Uncle Sam tapped on David's shoulder, Beth was expected to be strong, supportive, and prepared to carry on alone.

Uncle Sam did call, but not for combat. After 28 months in the California desert, David received orders for a two-year accompanied tour to the Marine Corps Detachment at Guantanamo Bay Naval Base, Cuba. David was relieved that his beloved wife was allowed to move with him.

"This was very rare at that time in the Marine Corps," David said. "Most tours were one year unaccompanied, meaning the Marine was sent without his or her family along."

At this point, tensions were high between Cuba and the United States. The on-going Cold War added pressure for David, who served as the Ground Defense Force Tanks Platoon Commander in Cuba. It was God's provision that the Marine Corps did not order David to leave his spouse behind.

Devastating news was about to slap them in the face, and Beth would desperately need David by her side.

❁ ❁ ❁

Shortly before their move, Beth started having sharp abdominal pains. She visited a chiropractor who discovered that she had, "a large lump that did not belong." Busy packing for Guantanamo, Beth didn't have time to wait for an appointment with a military doctor. She was 27 years old and healthy – surely the problem would resolve itself.

Yet her health worsened after they arrived in Cuba. The base doctor examined her and determined that her right kidney was enlarged and hard. Time was of the essence; they had to medevac her out of Cuba into a hospital on the mainland.

After extensive tests, doctors told Beth that she suffered from a rare and potentially fatal disease known as Tuberous Sclerosis. Both kidneys contained multiple benign tumors, of various sizes. The larger tumors were the most concerning: they could rupture spontaneously and cause Beth to bleed to death with little warning. Beth hadn't done anything to cause her condition — it was genetic. Beth wondered: how could *this* be part of God's plan?

Navy doctors monitored her condition, flying her back from Cuba for follow up exams and further testing as needed. Eventually the military moved the couple to Virginia Beach, VA., for David to attend the Marine Corps Intelligence School. It was a relief to be closer to advanced health care facilities. Both Beth and David felt uneasy knowing that at any moment, a ruptured tumor could threaten Beth's life. Their anxiety heightened when David left for his first oceanic deployment – he spent four months shipboard, part of a NATO exercise in Norwegian waters. Their separation was agonizing, especially for Beth.

"It was in the old days with no Internet and complete communication cut-off except for when the helicopters arrived with snail mail, usually three weeks after the mail was postmarked," David recalled. "It was a new experience for both of us."

Not only had Beth's health situation continued to fester, but she felt lonely with David so out-of-touch. Soon someone else joined the family: a fawn mutt with the wrinkles of a Shar Pei and the friendly nature of a Labrador Retriever. They named the adorable puppy Covert, falling in love with her big brown eyes and sheepish expressions. "She was an absolute joy in our lives," David said. "Covert was a godsend who needed a good home."

Yet even as Covert comforted them, Beth's illness tormented them. Several tumors had grown to a critical size, ticking like time bombs.

Six years into their marriage, Beth underwent her first surgery: the surgeon removed a tumor the size of a Nerf football. The doctor put the tumor in a bucket and carried it into the waiting room to show David and Beth's parents. They could hardly believe that *thing* had come out of Beth's body.

Yet the operation was only a temporary victory; in time dozens of new tumors would pop up, some growing to dangerous sizes. Beth would eventually lose her entire right kidney. Doctors stressed the seriousness of her condition, always fearful of a fatal bleed. She learned to cope with this sword of Damocles hanging over her head. "I chose not to worry about that," Beth said. "Over the years, it was a mental discipline thing."

Shutting out fear wasn't so easy for David; his wife's kidney disease revived oppressive memories of his father's demise and death. Despite his tough Marine training, David's anxiety spiked. He wasn't proud of feeling this way, but he acutely resented being forced to march down this horrifying road again. Before long, fate placed another boulder on David's shoulders: doctors advised Beth against becoming pregnant. Most likely, her body would not survive the stress.

❁ ❁ ❁

After absorbing this shattering news, Beth and David needed time to grieve. Neither could imagine a life without children. Eventually they reached what felt like an obvious decision: they would adopt. Soon they met with more heartbreak: they did not qualify. In the eyes of the adoption agencies, both parents carried unusually high rates of premature death. The mother could die at any moment from a burst tumor, and the father could fall in combat. Despite being loving, stable, and capable people, Beth and David were not considered a good risk to adopt an infant.

That rejection felt intensely personal. How unfair that many unsuitable, even abusive people became parents all the time while fate barred this devoted and loving couple from having a baby. After many tears and sleepless nights, Beth and David hatched a new plan. They would not give up on having kids. They were willing to adopt an older child from the foster system or embrace a child with special needs. Once again, the adoption agencies denied their request.

David was stung. "I was told I was good enough to go to war for my country but not good enough to be a father," he said.

Beth was outraged at the injustice: "I threw daily temper tantrums with God. I would scream, cry, and stomp my feet."

Soon the stress and resentment tore them apart. "We were both angry and took it out on each other," David conceded. Under the surface, he carried tremendous hostility. All he wanted was a normal life. Hadn't he already sacrificed his youth on the altar of devotion to another family member's illness?

"I didn't know if I could deal with this effectively, and I felt it was unfair to have to deal with it," David said. What's more, David was the only son of an only son – if he failed to have a child, his family name and bloodline would end with him. Beth felt personally responsible. At the same time, the terrible disease was not her fault, and she begrudged David for making her feel culpable.

"Many times, each of us thought, I am not liking this marriage, maybe we made a mistake, maybe we heard God wrong," Beth said. "Many years we had a lot of doubts."

Some days, the best reason for staying together came running to greet them with tail wags and welcoming licks whenever they walked through the front door. Covert was a unifying force in the family for 15 years. Both Beth and David felt the need to give their canine daughter a happy home.

Yet even the best of dogs cannot satisfy the primal longing for a child. The emotional distance between them widened; it felt as if they were stranded on opposite banks of a river while swollen flood waters pushed them farther and farther apart. They did not have enough skills or resources to redirect the rising waters or bridge the expanding gap. David felt cheated of being a parent while Beth felt cheated of unconditional love. Beth felt guilty for her illness while David felt guilty for resenting her. Neither one was happy.

At last, Beth waved a white flag. It was time to give up. "Maybe we need to go our separate ways," she said. "I'm done. You're done."

Without Beth, perhaps David could find another wife – a healthy one who would bear him children. He was not the one with the issue; there was still time for him to become a father.

"Yeah, we could split up…," David hesitated, before continuing, "but what would that do to the promise that we made to God, and to ourselves, the promise that we made in front of our family and friends?"

When David reflected deeply, it was the certainty of those first answered prayers, that deep sense that God had ordained their union, that kept him from running toward the nearest exit. They decided to hang on, in spite of their unhappiness.

"There are many times that I feel God put angels in our sight to block our view of being able to see a way out of this marriage," Beth says.

As happens in military families, Beth and David moved repeatedly. By their 30s, they were living in Alexandria, VA., and attending a large Baptist church. Everyone in their social circles was caught up in discussing childbirth, fertility, and baby stories.

In Sunday school, Beth and David took shelter in the company of three or four other couples who were also desperate to become parents. One by one, even those couples managed to join the elusive Baby Club, and Beth and David became completely isolated.

"Frankly, I got tired of hearing about other people's wombs," she said.

Wherever they had lived, Beth and David had relied on their church communities to provide an extended family network, but now they felt like odd balls. People wondered what was wrong with them. Why didn't they have kids? Some pitied them, others whispered behind their backs. Without realizing it, most of the young mothers were driving nails into Beth's wounded heart with their constant chatter about babies, babies, babies.

"Some of this felt very mean, very exclusionary," Beth said. "There is no space in the church for couples without kids – there are a lot of messages in church couched in that."

Mother's Day and Father's Day became unbearable; they avoided these Sunday services which focused on the blessing of children. Beth and David did not begrudge others this happiness, but such celebrations left them with an empty ache, like the starving beggar on the street corner who watches clusters of contented diners through the cafe window.

Maybe, just maybe, God would send a miracle their way. Perhaps somehow, a child needing a good home would appear in their lives, or an unconsidered avenue would reveal itself. But no door into parenthood opened. Despite tears and prayers, they remained bereft of children.

Despair and depression settled over them like a gloomy fog. Beth wished she could have spared David this burden, yet she yearned for his love and support to endure her disease with its frightening uncertainties. The gap of unfulfilled needs widened between them, further eroding the intimacy of their relationship.

✿ ✿ ✿

In early March 1999, David shipped out for a long tour in Okinawa, Japan, as senior staff for a Marine Corps Expeditionary Unit – Special Operations Capable. This was a mobile, risky mission that could not accommodate families. Beth stayed behind in Northern Virginia. In Japan, David was allotted a single room on base but most of the time, it was empty.

"I only lived in that room for a little over four total months out of the fourteen gone," David said. "The other months I was on deployment throughout Asia such as to urban warfare training in Guam and for seven months aboard the amphibious assault ship U.S.S. Belleau Wood."

David missed the spiritual nourishment from his home church, so he ordered a One Year Bible and started reading it daily. Every year since, he has read it through, gleaning something new. He says the discipline of this reading has helped keep his natural self in check. "I knew I could always go back to being that menace," he said. "It was an everyday decision to be that mentor. I was nothing more than a junkyard dog saved by grace."

David also tried to make daily contact with his wife. Communication methods had improved since his first deployment; they could usually connect unless David was tangled up in a mission, doing who knew what, who knew where. "I spoke with Beth once per week and exchanged emails — sometimes daily and sometimes hourly — while on ship," David said.

It wasn't nearly enough, yet Beth carried on. Some years earlier, she had completed her master's degree, and now she ran a thriving private practice as a family counselor. Work kept her busy, as did friendships, but without children or extended family in the D.C. area, Beth had empty time on her hands. She remembered how much the Singles Group had once meant to her, so she started teaching the current crop at church.

At last she had found a group whose lives did not revolve around raising children. Even so, she was not quite one of them. She was still the outsider, a married woman who was often alone.

"It was a tough year," Beth said.

On the medical front, the news was bad: the tumors in her remaining kidney had grown to an alarming size. Her doctor wanted to remove her only kidney and do a transplant. And if her body rejected the transplanted kidney, what then? She could die, her doctor informed her. After prayer and preliminary online research, Beth felt uneasy about this radical course. She asked the surgeon to give her a month to research other treatments.

"I hope you don't bleed to death in the meantime," he stated.

Undaunted, Beth found another doctor who was willing to take out the tumor and spare the host kidney through a novel and complicated surgery. That summer, her surgical team used radiation to shrink the tumor. Next, they cut off blood flow to the tumor. The following day they operated and took out the tumor with a flank incision.

David's superior officer would not grant him leave to come home from Asia. For Beth's sake, David regretted missing the surgery, yet when he was entirely honest with himself, he realized that he was also relieved. He wasn't keen on enduring the tense hours of sitting in yet another surgical waiting room while his unconscious wife lay hooked up to ventilators on yet another operating table. For better or for worse, he had orders to remain in Japan. It was easier for him to engage from a distance.

In the D.C. area, members of the Singles Group rallied around Beth. "They were as loving and supporting as they could be," she said. "It was a big two-day surgery, and the group decided to spend 24 hours in prayer. People took time off work to pray for me."

The surgery was successful, but it left Beth with a tremendously itchy scar from the 12-inch incision, as well as throbbing pain whenever she moved her core. Her energy levels were low; she felt old and weak. Months later when David finally returned home from his exhausting tour, he wanted someone to take care of him and help ease his transition back into ordinary life. But his wife was faltering. "Beth was just visibly not the same," David said.

"He was smacked in the face with the situation," she said. Although she hadn't fully recovered from her previous surgery, Beth underwent yet another operation a year and a half later. This time, the cumulative effect of anesthesia from five different surgeries left her with memory lapses. Several months later, Beth completely forgot David's 40th birthday.

David tried to understand. Gifts certainly weren't everything. But it hurt that his own wife had failed to acknowledge that he was entering a new decade. That Christmas, Beth did remember David mentioning that he needed rain gear, and she gave him a black golf umbrella. David was pleased until she purchased an identical umbrella for his birthday in April. She didn't even realize her mistake. For David, the duplicate umbrella spotlighted the issue. The strong, capable woman he had fallen in love with had been replaced by a fragile, forgetful version of Beth.

David was traumatized to see his wife slipping, yet he was also sorry for himself. "Because my father died when I was 18, his deteriorating medical condition during my high school years significantly impacted my upbringing," David said. "Beth's going through the same thing compounded my anger at having to go through this all over again."

Next came the shock of Sept. 11, 2001; as the airplane hijackings and terror attacks struck that morning in New York City and Washington, David was working at the Pentagon.

"I arrived at the outside of the building impacted by the airplane before the first responders arrived," he said. After the dust settled, everyone remained on high alert for months, wondering if another attack was coming.

"D.C. was tense at that time," David said. "Plus, we had the D.C. sniper shootings that next year, and the Anthrax in the postal mail." Such threats kept David tight as a coiled spring, intense, watchful and ever ready to pounce, exacerbating his visceral reactions at home.

To top it off, David's mother received a grim diagnosis of advanced leukemia. She passed away three weeks later. Then their beloved dog, Covert, died of kidney failure. "Of all things," David said.

It was a toxic mix. All traces of tenderness and empathy vanished from their home; isolation and anxiety took up residence instead. "We were not doing well together," Beth said. "We were tiptoeing around each other. We had a lot of resentment, a lot of anger."

For years, they had struggled to stem the loss of blood in their wounded marriage because it had seemed like the morally right thing to do. *Just keep the patient alive.* Now Beth was worn out from the trauma of trying to manage the crisis. Something in her spirit had reached a breaking point: "One day I said I'm done," Beth said. "Either you get help and we fix this, or I'm done. I am not going to live like this anymore." With her new clarity, Beth laid out her conditions for a continued relationship: David must undergo intensive therapy to deal with the trauma of his childhood. After some consideration, he came back with an answer: "I'll do whatever it takes."

David was not certain whether therapy would save their marriage. "I knew the end result would be whatever God's design was," he said. "But I was bound and determined, even if we divorced, that I would continue to love her. I wanted to make sure of that, whether we stayed together, or we split up."

Either way, his own instincts confirmed that Beth was right: the wreckage of his past needed hauling away. David threw himself into the therapy, opening up the locked closets of his memories, taking notes during sessions, and reflecting on whatever issues he'd uncovered. "I've never seen anyone work as hard at therapy as he did," Beth said.

His courage paid off. In the end, David was able to bury the ghosts of his father's slow demise and step into the present with more peace. As he and Beth gingerly discussed their future, they still felt God calling them to live together as husband and wife.

Only one thing remained to resolve, and it was the bravest surrender life would ever require of the competitive, hard-edged Marine. In a final act of submission before his sovereign Lord, David released his longing to be a father into God's hands. For years he had felt entitled to have a son or a daughter. Now, David would unquestioningly accept God's decision "if not having children, if not having a family of our own, was part of His training for us."

In his mind, David imagined tearfully leaving his coveted son wrapped in a blue blanket on God's altar. Would God, as with Abraham, accept the capitulation as a sufficient sacrifice and bless David with the gift of a son?

In the end, no child would appear in their world, but David would cease wailing against this injustice. God would honor David's contrite spirit with the gift of sufficient grace to accept his fate. His newfound serenity allowed Beth to lay down her guilt and move forward toward healing. At last, they could begin to put their grief behind them and focus on the many blessings that they had in one another.

✿ ✿ ✿

After 22 years as an officer in the Marines, David retired. Before launching into a new job, David took Beth on a long trip to Australia and New Zealand. They enjoyed the thrill of driving on the opposite side of the road, staying in quaint hotels and Bed and Breakfasts, and touring sun-dappled vineyards. For the first time in years, they felt as carefree as a couple of honeymooners.

"We had a marvelous time," Beth recalled. The extended trip helped them to relax, to laugh, to bond.

Afterwards, David went to work for the F.B.I. while Beth continued her counseling practice in the D.C. area. With David retired from the Marines, his deployments were over; they were able to live together every day and focus on creating a more positive relationship. In general, life was easier now. Their peers were no longer obsessed with their adorable youngsters. In fact, now that some of those cute kids had morphed into rebellious adolescents, Beth found new reasons to feel thankful for being childless. Their lives were certainly less complicated. And calmer! Beth and David would always regret not being able to raise a family, but the visceral pain had softened into a dull ache. Beth and David turned their focus outside of themselves, believing that God had other things for them to do.

Throughout their marriage, they have volunteered as a couple in countless ways to serve God, either on a Marine base or in church; in 2006, they spent two years developing the greatest legacy of their Christian work, Marriage Mentors United. This intensive program covers 19 exercises in areas such as family guidelines, finances, relationship goals, and unhealthy emotional baggage. The class trains happily married couples to work as mentors to young married couples within a church. Their Bible-based program is currently used in numerous churches in the D.C. area and in Charleston, S.C. Many hundreds of couples have benefited from their work.

"We're impacting the world for Jesus Christ one Christian marriage at a time," David said. He hopes the lessons learned from the breadth and depth of their experiences will encourage others to build a loving relationship.

"A great marriage doesn't get handed to you – a great marriage has got to be earned," David said. "You earn things by working hard at them." Beth agrees.

"We make it a point to have a lot of fun together," she says. "We are very open to having verbal praise. We talk about how much we like each other and how much we enjoy each other." Every night after dinner, they snuggle together on the sofa and relax. They enjoy taking walks in the park, having dinner with friends, exploring new places – and of course, serving God as a team.

In her 50s, Beth has now entered a safer phase of life. Tumors such as hers rarely rupture once a woman enters menopause. "I am really in pretty good shape these days," Beth said. "Even David is not worried about me anymore."

"For the first time since I was nine years old, I don't feel like I have the world on my shoulders," David says. They've made it, and Beth is grateful.

"David is so good for me: he helps keep me grounded," she says. "I am happy being married to this amazing man. I thank God every day for putting us together."

❊ ❊ ❊

For Group Discussion

1. How did Beth and David determine that they should wed?

2. Their hearts were filled with romantic notions as they prepared for their nuptials. Yet what lay in store for them?

3. What was the initial report on Beth's ongoing abdominal pain?

4. How did this change her expectation for her future?

5. Beth wondered how a genetically inherited, life-threatening disease could be part of God's plan. When have you experienced such questions? What helped you to work through your doubts?

6. As Beth underwent a series of dangerous surgeries, how did she cope with the stress?

7. As a teen, David had been the main caregiver for his father, who suffered diminished health due to chronic kidney failure. How did he respond to his wife's kidney-related illness?

8. What further blow did the doctors hit them with? Why was this especially painful?

9. What happened when Beth and David tried to adopt an infant? What happened when they tried to adopt an older child?

10. How did they each initially receive this news that adoption agencies considered them too high risk to be parents?

11. How did the prospect of being childless change their relationship?

12. After several years of misery, what did Beth finally suggest to David?

13. David considered his options; what made him stick it out in his marriage?

14. How did the Church and its communities help Beth and David

as they moved around the country with the military? Why did they eventually feel out of place amongst their peers at church?

15. Have you ever felt left out or different from the expectation of others, and why is this especially hurtful in a church setting?

16. While Beth and David prayed and waited for a miracle, no child appeared in their lives. How did this affect their treatment of one another?

17. What did David discover about his wife after he returned home from his tour in Japan? How did he react?

18. What additional stressors came into play for David and Beth after the terrorist attacks on Sept. 11, 2001?

19. What ultimatum did Beth finally lay down? Does God want us to endure chronic hostility from a spouse in order to uphold the sanctity of marriage?

20. How can people establish healthy boundaries for themselves?

21. David wasn't sure if their marriage could be saved; why did he agree to go to therapy? How did he approach his therapy sessions? What was the result of his therapy?

22. What final offering did God require David to make? How did this change David's outlook about what he was entitled to have?

23. What work did God call David and Beth to undertake as a team? How did their years of suffering prepare them for this ministry?

24. Consider David's statement, *a great marriage doesn't get handed to you. A great marriage has got to be earned.* How can this perspective prepare the soil for deeper intimacy to grow between a husband and wife?

25. In thinking back over the story, what was the major turning point for both Beth and David in their relationship?

Reflection

"Come to me, all you who are weary and burdened, and I will give you rest."
Matthew 11:28

"For we are God's handiwork, created in Christ Jesus to do good works, which God prepared in advance for us to do."
Ephesians 2:10

David and Beth endured their trials and worked to change themselves because of their desire to please God and to serve Him as a team. Likewise, if we lean into our faith, God will give us strength in difficult situations to grow in grace and love. As Isaiah 40:29 promises: "He gives strength to the weary and increases the power of the weak."

Claim this promise for areas of your life that need divine help. Understand that God opens the floodgates of compassion and healing to those who sincerely seek Him. What that healing looks like will be determined by God, but He will perform a mighty work wherever He is invited to enter. Be prepared to follow His nudges as He leads you onto a higher path.

Room for Your Thoughts & Observations

CHAPTER *SIX* / The Pastor's Wife

"She was rubbing that spot in me that was hurting."

Roberta & Roger married Aug. 17, 1974

I *feel like* I'm going to faint, Roberta thought, willing herself to recover. After the sudden wooziness had passed, Roberta felt too weak to keep standing and singing. She crept down from the choir risers as quietly as possible, trying not to disrupt the practice.

She fanned her hand in front of her face, indicating to the choir director that she was going to slip out for a breath of air. He nodded dismissively. It was a hot and sticky summer morning along the sandy coast of South Carolina; the heat could do things to people.

On the shady porch of the church, Roberta felt steadier. She hated ducking out of the choir warm up, but she honestly did not feel well enough to perform in the upcoming worship service. For days, Roberta had been off kilter in some indefinable way.

Was she exhausted? Was she sick? She shot up an internal prayer: *please God, help me understand what is going on with me.*

Clusters of people were gathered on the wide porch before the service; there was Roger, her husband. As usual, he was holding a Styrofoam cup of coffee in one hand and gesturing with the other, chatting in that endearing way of his. Cherie, the young and pretty wife of their pastor, was beaming up at him, poised to laugh at the punchline of his unfolding joke. Roberta and Roger were close friends with Cherie and Pastor Jim. Roberta waited for the joke to close before breaking in.

"Honey, I am not feeling well," she said. "I need you to take me home."

Home lay a half hour away at the end of a green tunnel of palmettos and live oak trees along S.C. 17, the state coastal highway. Roger always drove them to church in his GMC pickup. Sitting beside him in the cozy cab, Roberta opened up to her husband of 30 years. She tried to describe the internal sense of dread that had been creeping around in her head. Roberta had learned long ago to pay attention to her gut, examining her intuitions under the lens of the Bible. What was her Heavenly Father telling to her now?

Roger patted her hand. Everything was fine, he reassured her. This anxious feeling would pass. She was healthy and strong; she just needed a little rest. His soothing words took the edge off Roberta's fear. But not for long.

Minutes after they arrived home, a repugnant secret would reveal itself: amorous emails between Roger and Cherie. As Roberta read those atrociously affectionate words typed by her own husband, she felt nauseated.

Was Roger actually capable of this kind of duplicity? All those recent times when he had rubbed her aching feet, when he had joked around in his boyish way to win her smile, when he had brought her a cup of coffee in bed — was all of that a sham? No! Roger loved her; she knew he did. At least, she had believed it. Until now.

Tears filled Roberta's eyes as she reread Roger's message to Cherie: "Words can't describe how good it felt to hold you." She forced herself to take her eyes away from Roger's computer.

Red, hot anger shot through her. Roberta had devoted her entire life to satisfying this man, fussing over his daily needs, comforts, and wants as though he were a prince. Sure, their relationship had its ongoing issue: Roger craved attention, and Roberta had never been capable of giving him enough rapt feminine adoration. But they had hashed through this problem countless times, both trying to make changes. Overall, they were knit together like the fingers of a baseball glove.

Another woman? It did not seem possible.

Yet Roger's email said otherwise.

❁ ❁ ❁

The moment he had laid eyes on 17-year-old Roberta at a high school basketball game, Roger had been interested; yet blue-eyed, dark-haired Roberta was so pretty that Roger was afraid to ask for her home phone number, a decision he would later regret. It was still decades before mobile phones or social media. They lived 50 miles apart among corn fields and cow pastures in rural South Carolina, and the teens had few occasions to run into one another.

To make matters worse, Roger's parents were always dragging him over to their Pentecostal Holiness Church; not only did they attend services three times a week, but they went out of their way to spend time socializing with the pastor and other church leaders.

One weekend, a guest preacher from a neighboring county was speaking from the pulpit. Naturally Roger's parents had invited the visitor and his family out to Sunday dinner after the service. Roger and his three brothers were required to go along and help entertain them.

Imagine Roger's surprise when the striking girl with the baby-doll blue eyes turned up at the meal; who would have believed that Roberta's father was the guest preacher?

Joy of joys! For once his parents' churchiness had done him a huge favor. Roberta also remembered Roger; at their earlier meeting, she had enjoyed his humorous, boisterous personality. During the family meal, she decided he was handsome, with an expressive face and lively eyes. "We fell in love immediately," Roberta said. "We had very strong chemistry."

The attraction may have been the pull of opposites; in some ways, they were an unlikely couple. Roberta was a responsible girl who sewed her own clothes, worked a weekend job while keeping up good grades, and practically skipped to church three times a week.

"I was a lot more rowdy," Roger said. "I was involved in everything teenage boys get involved in."

He knew Roberta wouldn't approve of his drinking beer or

racing around in his truck on the local blacktop highways. As often happens, the hope of charming a lady transformed the young man. "I started behaving a lot better because I knew continuing to be rowdy wouldn't get me anywhere with her or with her family," Roger recalled.

Young and in love, they found themselves in passionate kissing sessions. Roberta was committed to being a virgin bride; Roger respected her morals. They got married soon after high school, when she was 18 and he was 19. After the initial ecstasy of physical intimacy, they had to figure out the hard task of daily living. When their two worlds merged, the transition was jarring.

"I hated church growing up. I despised everything about it," Roger said. "My life goal was to stop going. Then I married Roberta, Miss Goodie Two Shoes."

Roberta insisted that they attend church on the schedule laid out by their parents — twice on Sunday and again on Wednesday evening. If that wasn't enough to spoil things, Roberta had to be at her office job by 7:15 a.m., so she was asleep most nights by 9:30 p.m.

"He thought I was boring, but he didn't have to get up early," Roberta recalled. Roger ran his own handyman business. He installed carpeting, hung wallpaper, painted, and did other odd jobs, so his work hours were flexible. He felt cramped by his wife's rigid schedule.

Roberta expected them to sit down for a meal together at six every evening. That's what she had known growing up. Yet Roger had grown up in a bustling household where someone was always coming and going; it was natural for friends to pop over to shoot hoops or hang out, and folks grabbed food out of the fridge or the crock pot whenever they got hungry. No one was required to come to the table at a set hour.

Like children on a seesaw, the newlyweds moved up and down in reaction to one another, trying to establish their own balance as a fledgling family. On top of the petty squabbles, Roberta worried about a more serious problem.

"We weren't thriving spiritually," she said.

✿ ✿ ✿

Heaven and earth would shift for Roger on Sunday, Sept. 28, 1974. They went to morning church as usual. By late afternoon, Roger was feeling cranky about having to return for the evening service. He wanted to stay home and listen to a radio talk show about his beloved Carolina Gamecocks.

Like most guys in his hometown, Roger obsessed over South Carolina football. What defensive strategy might they employ next weekend to take out their opponent's star running back? Roger would much rather hear about college football than sit through another hum-drum sermon. Yet the scornful look on his young wife's face convinced him not to attempt the quarterback sneak to get past her. He was trapped.

When they arrived back at the church, an elderly neighbor came over and asked if they would drive her home; she wasn't feeling well. "I saw this as my chance to leave," Roger said.

Yet Roger felt a strange feeling wash over him while taking the neighbor home. "I told Roberta, we are going back to church. She was all for it," Roger said. "It was the Holy Spirit moving on the inside of me."

The sermon was half over by the time they had slipped into open seats near the back of the sanctuary. Roger doesn't remember a word the preacher said, but he will never forget what happened. In an uncharacteristic move, the pastor made an altar call. Roger felt stirred up. "It was as if someone grabbed me by the back of the neck and I just jumped up and almost ran down to that altar," he said. For the first time in his life, Roger wanted to connect with God. Emboldened by his example, three other men followed him down front.

When Roger knelt by the altar, the minister started praying over him with gusto. "No one had said anything to me about accepting Christ," Roger said. The prayer session ended. Roger went and sat on the front row. Before long, the pastor asked him to stand up and give his testimony – what had God done for him?

"Honestly, I don't feel any different than when I came down here," he confessed. Everyone was shocked. That was not the right answer.

"I was supposed to have been saved," he said. "Immediately the pastor and deacons grabbed me and went back to the altar and began praying."

It was like having a knot of Native Americans performing a rain dance around him as he knelt in prayer. The commotion of the ritual was unintelligible to Roger. What was he supposed to do? While the pastor and deacons continued to flutter their hands and offer intercessions, Roger's fifth grade teacher came over and whispered in his ear: "Ask God to help you repent. Ask Christ to come into your life."

Roger trusted her voice and opened his heart to Jesus. "When I got up, I knew I was different," he said.

Roger was a genuine believer now. He began praying and reading the Bible on a regular basis. He started going over to the church after work and sitting alone to spend time in prayer. In all those years of being dragged to worship services, he had never felt like this. Roger had developed a ravenous hunger to know God.

"When Roger does anything, he does it with his whole heart," Roberta said. "Because he was a Christian now, he was like, I am in this."

❄ ❄ ❄

Several years passed and eventually, life led them to Immanuel Bible College in Northeast Georgia. Roger was enrolled as student, and Roberta was raising the first of their brood.

Like many young brides, Roberta would ruminate over the little spats or slights that sprang up between them. "Whatever hurt Roger had inflicted on me, I would find it playing over and over again in my head," she said. "But love doesn't keep a record of wrongs. You can't move past something as long as you're dwelling on it."

During these tender years, Roberta felt challenged to practice the pure and unselfish love found in 1 Corinthians 13. "This was not necessarily love given to the person who sits next to you in church every Sunday, that's easy," Roberta said. "The Lord said I want you to apply it to the person who you live with every day – your husband."

Roberta wrote down the love chapter and plastered it on the bathroom mirror, in the car, all over their apartment. "Every thought you have, every idea you have, every word you say, I want you to measure it against this," the Holy Spirit told her.

Every day, Roberta practiced this lesson, yet despite her effort, she struggled to overcome a major issue in their marriage: the young bride could never make her husband feel special enough. As a child, Roger often felt like a slow learner in school. "Nobody knew what to do with me," he recalled. Like his father, a successful home builder, Roger was a natural with tools and excelled at building. But book learning was another story!

His academic challenges, coupled with the death of a younger sibling, had planted seeds of anxiety in Roger during his adolescence. He craved constant reassurance. "I never felt worthy, never felt loved," Roger said. "Roberta could never do enough to make me feel loved. She tried. She put forth as much as anyone possibly could to make me feel the love that was missing."

Roger thirsted for affectionate words and on-going praise, but Roberta had a more practical way of expressing her feelings. "I tried to show him I loved him by acts of service," she said. "I bent over backwards and did whatever I could do so that he had what he needs. I tried to protect him from whatever he didn't like. It's my way of saying I love you. He'd say I see that, but it doesn't satisfy my deepest needs."

Roberta wasn't sure what else she could do to make her man completely happy. After Bible college, they returned to the midlands of South Carolina where Roger had two careers: home building and pastoring at a Pentecostal church on weekends. A full-time wife and mother of four, Roberta continued to try and love her husband by the high standard of 1 Corinthians 13: love is patient, love is kind, love wants the best for the beloved.

Yet Roger remained frustrated in his quest for emotional intimacy. "Roberta is one of the finest people I have ever known," he said. "She cooked meals and just plain spoiled me. She got me ruined. But she is not very affectionate. She doesn't know how to move in my world with me and that is what I have always wanted. My understanding of marriage is to be one. I want her to look in my face and say things that her heart is speaking. Even though she tells me that she loves me, it's like there's this void there."

Roberta felt that her husband was asking more than she could sincerely rouse. "I had tried to give him what he wanted, and I felt unable to do it," she said. "I told him that I felt like I am never going to be the person who satisfies you in this way. And he would say, 'I've told you what I need. It's not impossible. This tells me that you don't love me.'" They lived with the unresolved issue, hoping to find an answer.

Each was doing his or her best to build a happy family and live according to Biblical standards.

No one looking at their relationship from the outside could have perceived the hair-line fracture.

✿ ✿ ✿

Time passed and, after 25 years of marriage, Roger was able to fulfill one of Roberta's lifelong dreams. She had always wanted to live at the beach, and a business opportunity enabled them to move to a charming town on the Carolina coast. By now, Roger had a successful home design career and Roberta worked part-time as a real estate appraiser.

They were still unpacking boxes when an emotional earthquake shook their family. One of their nieces revealed that their oldest daughter, Randi, 17, had been a victim of chronic sexual abuse. For more than a decade, an older male cousin had molested and raped Randi as well as the niece. Randi had been too ashamed to tell anyone, but now her heinous secret was out.

Randi wasn't prepared to deal with the exposure. Roberta and Roger tried to help, but Randi rejected them and their faith. Randi sought refuge in drinking and drugs, eventually latching onto the dangerous and highly addictive methamphetamine, or meth. Randi gave into despair and her life spun out of control. Drug dependency enslaved her.

Roberta orchestrated an intervention: all the important people in Randi's life came together and pleaded with her to get help. Moved by the show of concern, Randi agreed to seek treatment. Eventually she would recover and establish a meaningful career in Christian mission work. But for several years, Roberta poured her energy into rescuing and supporting Randi. She had even less patience for her husband's neediness now.

"I was consumed in trying to save my daughter's life," Roberta recalled. "I reached the point where I looked at Roger and said, 'You need to be happy, and I can't seem to fix it. God knows I have tried. You just married the wrong person. Get on out there and see if you can find that person and if you do, I will release you.'"

Her words were spoken out of frustration. Roger knew she didn't mean it.

But someone was waiting, eager to step into Roger's heart: the pastor's wife. Despite having three young children, Cherie was only a few years older than Roger and Roberta's oldest daughter. "Getting attention from a younger woman, it's very flattering – if you have an image problem, it is very difficult to walk away from that," Roger said.

Cherie was pretty in a frilly, girly sort of way, with blonde, curly hair and a warm smile; Cherie was affectionate by nature and hungry for affirmation. Roberta and Roger had a tradition of befriending their pastors and their families: they took them to dinner, bought gifts for their kids, and looked for little ways to make their lives more pleasant.

"I think Cherie was totally misreading some of that. Her husband was married to the ministry, and she was needing more attention. It was the perfect set up," Roberta explained. "It started very casually; they would call each other or answer each other's emails or texts. It was not unusual for any one of the four of us to shoot a friendly email."

No longer an active pastor, Roger was employed full-time as a contractor in home construction. Yet he served as a church deacon, working closely with Pastor Jim. The two families spent plenty of time together — boating, going out for fried shrimp and oyster platters, or simply sitting in the back yard relaxing on weekends. An obvious attraction developed between Roger and Cherie. They would openly catch each other's eye, exchange mischievous smiles, and banter back and forth. "It was so ridiculous that my children called her my girlfriend," Roger said.

Roger figured their flirtations were harmless. "I told myself it's not dangerous because you're too old," he said. "She would never be interested. That was a lie."

Things eventually crossed into a murky area. Roger began thinking about Cherie at odd moments. But he never acted on his impulses to take things further until Cherie started sending more personal messages. *What are you doing? How is your day going?*

"Before long, you are saying things you know you shouldn't be saying, like you sure do look pretty today," he said. Soon enough Cherie was discussing her marital problems. She let Roger know that her husband made her feel unwanted and unattractive.

"As a man, it feeds you into thinking, I would know what to do about that," Roger said.

Trying to help, Roger prodded his pastor. "Behind the scenes, I am telling him you really need to notice your wife. He'd just kind of shrug it off. It's no problem. But I'd say don't treat her that way, don't talk to her that way."

One afternoon on the boat, Cherie propped her leg up on her husband's lap; seeming annoyed, Pastor Jim quickly pushed her away, saying, "Don't touch me. It's too hot out here."

Roger flinched, then he glanced at Cherie, furtively communicating with his eyes, "You deserve better." He wanted Cherie to know: he would never treat her like that. Yet, he was completely conflicted. Roger adored his wife and his family. "It was never about a future together or about getting into a sexual relationship," he said.

Cherie was irresistible for different reasons.

"She was rubbing that spot in me that was hurting," he said. "She was meeting a need in me that I had, and I was meeting a need that she had. Her husband was ignoring her."

No one realized that something serious was growing behind the games. "She just emailed him one day and said, 'I think I am falling in love with you,'" Roberta said. "It kind of just exploded in him. Just hearing those words, everything changed."

Roger and Cherie yearned for one another. He would read and re-read her emails, basking in the warmth of her compliments. Cherie was offering the Holy Grail of emotional intimacy that had long been Roger's quest. And yet, Roger felt guilty. He dropped clues to his wife.

"I'm saying things to Roberta indicating that I am too close to Cherie," he said. "Cherie would tell me things that were personal, like how many times they had sex, and I would turn around and tell Roberta." Roger sensed the attraction might be approaching a crescendo. He should end it before things became physical or one of their spouses discovered their notes. "We can't go on like this," he told Cherie.

But neither was willing to walk away.

Roger met Cherie for lunch at a local diner. When they ran into a friend from church, they acted nonchalant, as if they were discussing plans for a new Sunday school program. No one seemed suspicious, so a few weeks later, they met again.

After this second lunch, they got into Roger's truck to take a ride and talk privately. They ended up parking on a dead-end road in the middle of a forest. No one was around. Casually, Cherie stretched out her hand on the bench seat, resting her fingers mere inches from his thigh. Before long, they were wrapped in a desperate embrace, kissing with abandon. Cherie collapsed willingly into Roger's arms, her soft hair tickling his neck; Roger sensed that she was ready to be swept off her feet.

Roger cared for Cherie, and for months he had longed to show her the way a real man would treat her. She was a beautiful woman who deserved to be appreciated. Everything about holding her — the scent of her skin, her petite frame, her long blonde hair — felt unfamiliar and exciting. For 30 years, Roger had been coupled with only one woman. Now he was putting his face against the soft cheek of someone new.

"That was the picture of wonderful and nasty," Roger recalled. "It felt awful to be doing that with another woman, and yet — the Bible says, sin feels good for a season."

Roger's moral policeman was yelling in his brain. *Stop before it's too late! What are you thinking?* Roger pulled away, telling Cherie that he was too much of a gentleman to take advantage of her in a rash moment. They needed to get their rushing emotions under control before they were carried over the edge.

The strongest magnet that pulled him toward Cherie was not sexual desire. "Roberta and I had a great sex life," he said. "This thing with Cherie was emotional. She looked me in my eyes and said what I wanted to hear. It was more than I could overcome."

"He kept going back because it was so exhilarating," Roberta said.

❀ ❀ ❀

A few days after Roger and Cherie embraced, Roberta began to sense that something was wrong. The disquiet peaked the day she felt faint at church. Although Roberta did not realize it, church was no longer a sanctuary but the place where a rival was batting her eyelashes and displaying her feminine charms. Like a tripped burglar alarm, Roberta's intuition was warning her to get away.

As fate would have it, their daughter Randi had stayed home

from the worship service that morning. When Roger and Roberta walked through the kitchen door, Randi appeared on the brink of tears.

"Mama, I need to talk to you," Randi said. "Let's go somewhere." They drove down the street to have privacy.

"Honey, tell Mama what's wrong," Roberta said.

With a shaky voice, Randi explained: she had picked up her father's laptop while her parents were at church. When the computer sprang to life, the screen displayed an email from Cherie. Their pastor's wife had typed a mushy message about kissing Roger.

"Definitely stuff is going on," Randi told her mother.

Roberta reassured Randi that she had done the right thing in telling her. As she processed this shocking news, Roberta initially felt her anger pointed entirely at the other woman. *Why that hussy! After all the nice things I've done for her and her children!*

But that was irrational; she had to admit that Roger was guilty, too. Roberta felt as if she'd been kicked in the gut. Although it was absurd, she found herself grasping for a sliver of hope. Perhaps when she confronted Roger, he would be able to explain it all away. Instead, Roger hung his head and admitted his attachment to Cherie.

The ugly truth had been staring Roberta right in the face, but she had been too trusting to see it. Her intense sense of betrayal overwhelmed her. "It was the most powerful emotion I have ever felt," Roberta said. "I never even knew I could feel that kind of pain. It was deep, so deep. I can't even describe it. It was like somebody went down to the depths of my soul and just raped me."

She needed space to think. "Just leave," she told her husband. "I don't care where you go, just get out of this house."

Crumpled with shame, Roger retreated to the dependency apartment over the garage where Randi lived. By now Roger comprehended how foolish he had been; his impassioned thought life had led to this reckless course of action. Roger had ended up with Cherie in his arms after months of indulging in sensual fantasies and cultivating her desire for him. He had become smitten with another woman. He had betrayed his true love. He was unworthy of his wife.

"I've never been more broken in my life," he said. "My pain had as much to do with Roberta's pain as my own. I couldn't bear what I had done to her."

Roger emailed Cherie, explaining that their relationship had been discovered. He advised Cherie to talk with her husband before Pastor Jim heard the news from someone else.

Roger shut his computer; the room felt too lonely and quiet. The man who had craved constant attention now found himself absolutely alone. Roger cried out to God. He had ruined in his marriage and family life, and he needed someone to rescue him. In answer, God showed Roger a vision.

"In the vision was a treasure, and I let it drop and hit the floor," Roger said. "God said that is what you just did to your wife. But I am going to come to you. You're going to be as much restored as she is in pain."

Roger clung to that seemingly impossible promise. He didn't leave the studio apartment but toggled between self-loathing, sorrowful prayer, and restless sleep. "That was the longest afternoon and night of my life. It was horrific."

The next day, Roger walked over to the main house; he called his wife and children into the den and told them what God had shown him. "I will do whatever it takes to find a way to make this right," Roger said. "I will do whatever God prescribes or Roberta, you prescribe."

His genuine remorse touched a sympathetic place in Roberta, and she allowed him to continue to speak. "This is not what I wanted. I want you and I want my family," he reassured her. "I know I have to earn your trust and repair our relationship, but I will do it."

Roger felt he needed to ask for forgiveness from Pastor Jim. Cherie had confessed to her husband, but Roger wanted to do his part. "I am going to go and face him and be a man," he told Roberta. The two men sat in Roger's truck discussing the situation. "I've been telling you for months that your wife is starving for attention," Roger said. "When I'm gone, you will still have a wife that's lacking in that way."

To Roger's surprise, Pastor Jim was not hostile; he forgave Roger and invited him to come back to church and move forward as if nothing had ever happened.

✿ ✿ ✿

Yet for months, Roberta and Roger continued to avoid church; for different reasons, neither dared to face the other woman. Losing their church connection created an enormous vacuum in their social and spiritual lives. "We loved that church – we felt cheated out of our church family," Roberta said.

Even in her angriest moments, Roberta had told no one about the scandal; she felt it would be wrong to shame her husband. Friends and choir members kept asking why they had disappeared. Roberta offered vague excuses and vaguer promises of their eventual return. They found a family therapist and began working on their relationship. Eventually the therapist suggested that they return to church as a family and help one another deal with the ache and awkwardness. If they could handle that, "it would make an even bigger statement about faith and forgiveness," the counselor said.

Initially, the ordeal was almost more than Roberta could bear.

There was Cherie, dressed up and looking fetching in her Sunday clothes and acting the part of the perfect pastor's wife. Resentment scorched Roberta. "It was an exercise in sheer discipline for me not to blow up," Roberta confessed. "It was a painful reminder. We were stressing ourselves to the max even being there."

Each week when Roberta returned, her emotional reaction gave her a true reading of her progress toward forgiveness. "It was a gauge of where my inner man was in the process and of how murderous my thoughts were," she said. "I would think things like, I would love to see you hung up by your toenails. I would love to tell everyone what a whore you are! I kept facing it until eventually I could feel myself letting go. Every time I would let go a little, God would come in with a little bit more healing oil. It was a torturous ordeal."

Roger was working through a complicated grief. One part of him still mourned for the damage he'd inflicted on his marriage. Meanwhile, another part of him was having withdrawals from the excitement of Cherie's attention. "There were several days where, if Cherie had called me, I would have fallen back into it," he said. "I was an emotional wreck. Talking to her would have eased that pain."

He would soon have the chance. Two months after the affair had ended, Roger called Pastor Jim on his cell phone to discuss some church business. Cherie answered her husband's phone. Roger was not expecting to hear her voice. Shivers ran down his spine when she tenderly spoke the word hello.

"How are you doing?" he asked.

"I really miss you," she replied.

"I really miss you too," he said. A moment of silence passed between them.

"I still think about you all the time," Cherie confessed.

"Me too."

That was their last private conversation. Meanwhile, Roberta obsessively observed her husband, constantly asking where he'd been and if he was thinking about the other woman. She checked his emails; she read his text messages. She made him answer for every minute of his day.

"Where's your mind? Where's your heart? Where are you going?" she would ask.

"For a while, I had to know those things. He really did have to answer all my detailed questions. Are you still thinking about her? Are you driving through town (near her house)? I was torturing myself and torturing him," she said.

When pressed, Roger admitted that he was still musing about Cherie. "He was honest and when he said yes, it would hurt," Roberta said. "He knew what he had to do to live with himself and to live with me in honesty and truth, and he wanted that. This went on for several months, and then the Holy Spirit spoke to me and said you can never control Roger's behavior or his conscience – you are trying to police him. You cannot be his moral police. If you try to control him from the outside, you will not be happy with the end result. Let me work from the inside."

Roberta received this revelation while sitting in her favorite prayer spot, a private corner in her walk-in closet that contained a cozy window seat. Often, she would retreat here to journal, pray, and cry. Now she understood with clarity what she needed to do. With a determined stride, she walked out and found her husband sitting in his favorite chair in the den. "You don't answer to me anymore," she said boldly. "You answer to God. You're free from having to answer my questions."

His wife's sudden reversal astounded Roger. At last, Roberta was moving toward trusting him again. Roberta longed to be able to offer her husband full restoration; she wanted to be the 1 Corinthians 13 kind of wife with a love that forgives all. But she still needed a means of unloading her bitterness.

❊ ❊ ❊

For the next six months, Roberta filled page after tear-soaked page of her journals. She would often read over her words and re-live the painful drama. One day while she was absorbed in her diaries, Roberta sensed the Holy Spirit saying, "Are you ready?" Instinctively, Roberta understood.

Years earlier, she had heard a story about a woman burning painful letters and personal papers as a means of letting go. As if by divine suggestion, the memory of this appeared in her mind. After some deliberation and prayer, Roberta went outside and burned all the embittered journal entries. The orange tongues of fire consumed the diaries, turning them into piles of ash; Roberta felt indignation and self-pity fly away from her soul.

"It was a release for me," she said. "When this thing goes up in flames, I am letting it take all of this with it. I wanted out – I did not want to live there. I relied on the Holy Spirit during that time."

Energized to move on, Roberta looked for specific ways to build up her marriage. She and Roger would steal away to the park and swing; walk down to the beach holding hands; take a drive to nowhere, all the while talking and deeply connecting. "We checked in with each other.... how have you felt today? What have you been thinking?" They intentionally nurtured their relationship.

Roberta felt the Lord remind her that love covers a multitude of sins. She continued to protect her husband's reputation, resisting any temptation to share her hurt and anger with friends. "If you love him, you will cover him," she felt God say. "I have forgiven him. It's over."

When she needed to talk, Roberta hashed it out with Roger or cried out to the Lord. She refused to bad mouth her husband or Cherie. "What I learned from my daughter Randi's experience is that in life there are always two options for us as Christians," Roberta said. "We can walk in the flesh or we can walk in the spirit. I wasn't perfect but the Holy Spirit presented the challenge again and again. The Spiritual is always the higher road. It opposes the flesh. This brings the deepest healing possible."

Through the pain, Roger has gained a new understanding of forgiveness. To satisfy his deep self-image issues, Roger has learned to meditate on his position as a beloved child of a Heavenly Father. In his thoughts, Roger turns expectantly to God throughout the day. By seeking God first, Roger has attempted to live within the Kingdom of God while still on earth.

"If you are not astonished or amazed at your relationship with God, you are missing something," Roger said. "It's all about the relationship."

Years after their marital crisis, Roger almost died in June 2014 from a massive heart attack, followed by a stroke that impaired his ability to walk and talk. Roberta stayed constantly beside him throughout months of hospitalization and rehabilitation, loving him with such devotion that everything else in her life came to a screeching halt. Now home again, Roger lives with his biggest supporter and cheerleader, his wife. He has made miraculous strides in his recovery.

"This has made our love for each other stronger and sweeter," Roberta says. "It's just purer somehow." Roberta has finally become the 1 Corinthians 13 wife in every way.

❁ ❁ ❁

For Group Discussion

1. When Roberta felt anxious and unsettled enough to leave church, how did Roger respond? Did he manage to soothe her fears?

2. What terrible secret did Roberta discover after returning home? Had she been suspicious of her husband before this moment?

3. What on-going issue had plagued their long marriage?

4. As a young wife, how did Roberta train herself to love her husband unselfishly?

5. Despite Roberta's concerted efforts, why was Roger so needy?

6. How did Roberta demonstrate her love? How did Roger react to this type of giving?

7. What was it that Roberta could not dredge up? How did they deal with their marital tension?

8. How did Roger and Cherie's relationship begin? What was the joke about her in their family?

9. Why was Cherie hungry for attention?

10. Roger felt guilty about his emotional entanglement with Cherie; how did he subtly suggest this to his wife? Why didn't Roberta pick up on it?

11. What happened after Roger and Cherie began meeting for lunch?

12. What about Cherie made her irresistible to Roger? Perhaps you can remember a time when someone was paying you a lot of flattering attention. Can you relate to how Roger felt?

13. After the secret was out, how did Roger attempt to reconcile with Roberta? How did she respond?

14. Why did Roberta decide to keep silent about her husband's fling? Would you be willing to protect your spouse's reputation if he or she

had wronged you?

15. After a betrayal, it takes time to rebuild trust. How was Roberta treating her husband? What did the Lord say about this?

16. Why is it wrong to serve as another person's moral compass? How should we respond when we find ourselves trying to control others?

17. What did Roberta finally do to release her sorrow and bitterness?

18. How was Roger able to mature and overcome his emotional dependency? How did God bring good out of this painful mistake?

19. In thinking back over the entire story, what was the turning point for Roger? For Roberta?

Reflection

"Bear with each other and forgive one another if any of you has a grievance against someone. Forgive as the Lord forgave you."
Colossians 3:13

"See what great love the Father has lavished on us, that we should be called children of God! And that is what we are! The reason the world does not know us is that it did not know Him."
1 John 3:1

What do you base your sense of security upon? Like Roger, how can you draw a deeper sense of self-worth from the fact that God loves you beyond measure? How might this change the way in which you see yourself....and others? Try spending time each day in silent prayer, focusing on God's love for you as His precious child. Contemplate on how this is your true, and eternal, identity.

Room for Your Thoughts & Observations

CHAPTER *SEVEN*/Gambling on Love

"We didn't try to fight it."

Alice & Clint married Dec. 29, 1971, then remarried
Nov. 4, 1989

They **Met at work.** Clint was an engineer at a textile factory in the mountains of Tennessee; Alice sat at a reception desk in the adjacent administration building. It was only a fluke that placed them in the same room.

Sparks flew when Clint first spoke to Alice in his deep Johnny Cash voice. "Clint came be-bopping up the sidewalk. He had his *I don't give a damn* hat on and his confident way of walking," Alice recalled. "I liked the way he had a spring in his step. When he started talking and I heard that voice, I was done for...I thought, I want that man."

Wearing his canvas pork pie hat slightly askew, Clint greeted her with an amused, cocky grin. He stated his business — he had come to see her boss. Yet he didn't seem in any hurry to move on to the inner office. He made it clear that he liked what he was seeing at the reception desk. As Clint's mischievous eyes swept over her with an appreciative look, Alice felt an unexpected throb of attraction. He tossed up a few silly comments, trying to amuse her, and Alice found herself giggling. When Clint complimented her blouse, Alice felt her cheeks flush.

It's nice to feel pretty again. Alice lived with a man who constantly criticized her.

In the days that followed, Clint found excuses to return frequently to the office. He made it a point to let Alice know that he moonlighted as a bartender at a local tavern. Alice and her friends began hanging out there on weekends. Before long, Clint became her boyfriend.

"We didn't try to fight it," Alice said. "He was just as attracted to me as I was to him."

Their sexual union felt as unstoppable as a stampede of wild horses. Alice had a husband and three children, but she was easily seduced away from an unhappy marriage. Likewise, Clint was married with three kids, but he was restless and bored. The more time they spent together, the more the magnetism intensified.

"It just flamed," Alice said. "We just fit each other's needs. My marriage fell apart, and I saw a reason for leaving. I loved this other guy."

Alice left her first marriage when her youngest child was five years old. Her husband was outraged and tried to stop her. However, in Tennessee at that time, she could get a divorce within 24 hours because she had grounds of adultery. "Neither one of us had been faithful," she said.

As word spread about Alice and Clint's liaison, their employer terminated both of their jobs. Despite this, Alice and Clint did not regret their affair. They had cast off spouses and damaged relationships with their children to pursue their romance.

"We had fought so hard for each other, to be together, because this was a lifetime love," she said. As soon as they could manage the details, they married and moved to North Carolina.

Yet red-hot liaisons often burn out. Sixteen years into this second marriage, their relationship lay in shambles. Alice could reel off the reasons: unfaithfulness on both sides; gambling at poker by Clint; and heavy drinking. From the start, they'd both partied hard on the weekends, and Clint had always enjoyed his bourbon on the rocks. But now Clint drank excessively, and the whiskey brought out his mean streak.

"I knew that wasn't what I wanted for the rest of my life," Alice said.

Perhaps the meanness was the tipping point. Too often when Clint returned home frustrated after losing at cards, he attacked

157

Alice with a drunken barrage of insults. That rich, smoky voice had once wooed her; now Clint used it to wound her. Alice was utterly confused about whether or not her marriage could be saved.

Her feelings bounced around like a pinball, ricocheting from one extreme to the other: she should stick it out with Clint. She should leave him. Sometimes she felt divorce was the obvious choice, and yet — she did not want to fail at marriage a second time. By this point she was a middle-aged woman who had put on a bit of weight: if she left Clint, she feared spending the rest of her days alone. If only they could be happy again and rediscover the love they had once known.

Was that even possible?

❊ ❊ ❊

One fateful night Alice found her answer literally emblazoned across the dark sky over their golf course community. Alice and Clint lived beside the fairways in a condo, but she was staying with a friend for a few weeks to sort through her feelings about her husband.

Alice didn't tell Clint that she was coming back to their neighborhood to babysit for her grandchildren. Her daughter lived only a short stroll from the golf course. After the children were asleep, Alice slipped out for a walk over to their spot on the 10th Fairway. Her Oreo-colored cats were probably out on the patio.

Did Clint even remember to feed them? He'd never liked them. Alice had not been able to bring the cats with her to her friend's house. She yearned to see their adorable little faces; this hope propelled her forward on the golf cart path.

A chilly wind ruffled her hair. Alice looked up at the spread of silvery stars twinkling across the black horizon. She prayed to God for guidance. True, she'd never been a saint, but she needed help from somewhere. Soon Alice was peering at the outline of her former home. Her eyes took in the low, neat Pittosporum hedge surrounding the condo's patio. The floodlights were on, and the house was completely dark.

Clint must be out raising hell again. She shook her head.

Alice searched for her cats around the patio table and its four chairs. Not finding them, she crouched to peer under the flat-topped bushes. Her two furry boys were nowhere in sight. As she stood up to move on, Alice staggered before getting her footing. She was surprised to find herself engulfed by sorrow. Was she really this distraught about not finding her cats? No. Alice laughed under her breath: some part of her was cuckoo enough to still yearn for her husband. She felt empty without Clint.

He had betrayed her and hurt her, and yet ... she was more attracted to him than to any man she'd ever known. Lying against his broad chest and listening to Clint breathe made her feel complete. She even missed the comforting smell of his skin.

I will always love that man. There is no one else like him.

Turning her back on the condo, Alice shivered in the damp night air. She feared she would never feel such intense emotions again, but their passions had run too high, at times morphing from love into hate. She was bedraggled from fighting. For months, friends had been telling her that she'd be better off without Clint. *Tell that to my heart.*

Alice returned her gaze to the speckling of stars and cried out to the heavens: "Lord, is this the right thing? Should I divorce him -- and go my own way?"

As if on cue, a shooting star blazed across the dome of the sky. Alice watched intently, sensing her own destiny playing out before her eyes. Suddenly, the meteor did the most astonishing thing. During its course of flight, the trail of light unexpectedly split. The severed lines began rushing in opposite directions. Alice stood frozen, dumbstruck. The gap widened with every passing second until the bright lines burned out.

"I had never seen anything like that before," Alice recalled. "I was just like oh, okay! I guess I've got it."

Alice made a leap of faith; she officially separated from Clint and became a resident guest at a little monastery located nearby in a remote pine forest. As part of its mission, the Holy Savior Priory opened its wrought-iron gates to any weary soul seeking refuge. Her hermit's cottage reflected the vows of poverty taken by the monks: stark white walls and a cot with thin, cotton bedding.

"It was a holy place, a place where you were stripped of all your stuff, "Alice said.

Alice found peace among the brown-robed monks, their organic vegetable garden, and their head-bobbing, free range chickens. While the monks chanted, Alice sought strength and guidance from a mysterious God.

A few years earlier, Alice had begun feeling guilty about her adultery with Clint and the careless way they had ended their first marriages. She had even confessed her sins to a compassionate priest who had assured her of God's mercy. Yet such grace seemed too good to be true. Alice had been reared in a small mountain community where God was portrayed as an angry deity who sits in fiery judgment over sinners. Alice yearned to escape from feeling like one of the damned. But the roots of her fears ran too deep.

Alice had been tainted from birth.

❀ ❀ ❀

When Alice was only six months old, her mother had abandoned her and her older sister, Judith. "She had decided she did not want to be a mother anymore," Alice recalled.

Their unmarried mother had run away from disgrace and toward freedom. No one had ever taken responsibility for being their father, so the girl's maternal grandparents adopted them, despite their struggles to provide for their own children. Several of Alice's aunts and uncles still lived at home. Alice and Judith understood: they were more hungry mouths in a tiny house perched on the side of a mountain in Grundy, Virginia.

"It was not a happy childhood," Alice said.

Money was tight for Granny and Gramps, and supplies were

short: no car, no new clothes, no store-bought toys. Gramps scratched out a living as a blacksmith. His shop was tucked behind their house, but it was off limits to children. On days when Gramps was paid in moonshine for his horseshoes or augers, the smithy shop became a place for men to gather and drink. Better for young girls to stay away. If they annoyed Gramps, he might strike them.

"I can recall him slapping me across the face on our way back from someplace when we were walking home," Alice said. "He used to spank me with a razor strop. I was scared of the sight of shaved whiskers for many years."

As a young teen, Alice developed a temper. "Once I got angry about having to do the dishes when I was about 11 years old, and I slammed the cupboard door and broke it," she recalled. "There were times when I deserved a spanking."

The girls missed having parents who made them feel safe and cherished, although they were too proud to admit it. "I had a chip on my shoulder almost all of my life," Alice said. "I was like, I'm strong and I'm going to take care of myself."

Eventually their mother, now married and raising two small boys, returned to the area and moved to a neighboring town. She wanted to reestablish a relationship, but Alice and her sister had hardened their hearts against her. Every so often, Granny would force Alice and Judith to ride the public bus and go spend a few nights with their mother.

It felt unnatural, another awkward family group where they did not belong. To explain away her teenage pregnancies, Alice's mother began claiming that she had been raped. This story left Alice dripping in shame. In the isolated coves of their mountain community, being the byproduct of an unblessed union was akin to wearing a scarlet letter. No one believed her mother's excuses, and her presence had revived the scandal around Alice's and Judith's births.

"It was hard to get through middle school," Alice recalled. "Let me tell you, when I was 13 or 14 years old, I heard some things. My girlfriend said she was not allowed to play with me because I didn't have a daddy."

In Grundy, children paid dearly for the sins of their parents. "Where I grew up, if a baby was born deformed, people thought God was punishing them by giving them an imperfect child," Alice said. The local pastors ranted about a vengeful God. Is it any wonder people wanted to keep their daughters away from the fatherless sisters? Sometimes even Alice herself wondered if she were cursed.

One summer day in middle school, Alice and two friends were floating down a creek in inner tubes when a violent thunderstorm broke open. The girls needed to get out of the water.

They hopped to their feet and scurried across slippery rocks to reach the riverbank. Once on dry land, the girls scampered toward a friend's house with their inner tubes flapping under their elbows. Lightning walloped a nearby tree, knocking the girls to the ground. They clambered to their feet, leaving the tires behind to the roaring wind. They managed to reach the house and get inside; a few minutes later, Alice sat huddled on the family room rug, draped under the comfort of a towel. She was just beginning to calm down when — pop! A floor lamp exploded in her direction, striking the back of her neck with hot pieces of glass.

"I thought God was out to get me," she confessed.

❀ ❀ ❀

Alice's grandparents had never taken her to church, but among the superstitious coal miners and their wives, she'd heard plenty of talk about the threat of divine punishment. Church did not become appealing to the sisters until they were teenagers, eager to expand their social circles. Then Alice and Judith had begun walking to various Youth Groups, wanting to visit with friends — and flirt with boys.

At 16, Alice met a man who would eventually put flesh and bones on the image of the vindictive deity. Several years older, Weymouth was attending a community college. In the beginning, he seemed educated and dashing. They dated happily until disaster struck in the fall of Alice's senior year of high school.

Alice enjoyed team sports, and she had won the coveted spot as captain of the girls' basketball team. Her world changed forever when she discovered that she was pregnant. She tried to hide her condition, but after the baby bulge began to show, Alice was tainted by scandal all over again. The principal asked Alice to withdraw from school. She wasn't even allowed to finish the basketball season.

She and Weymouth discussed their options.

Alice refused to consider abortion, feeling it was morally wrong. Weymouth agreed, knowing what his daddy would say. Weymouth's father was a self-trained, Freewill Baptist pastor whose fiery orations drew in the poorest, least educated people. "They were hill people from up in the hollow," Alice said. "They did not have indoor plumbing; they had an outhouse." Weymouth was raised that women should never wear makeup or cut their hair. Neither men nor women should chew gum, smoke, drink alcohol, or go to the movies. Sex outside of marriage was taboo, and abortion was tantamount to murder.

Weymouth suggested they consider contacting adoption agencies.

Alice refused.

"You don't give a child up, because that had been done to me, and it wasn't a good thing," she said. That left only one option. Papa Price baptized Alice in the river before he married her to his son in a simple ceremony. "We were both too young," she conceded. "I was 18 and he was 21." Yet Weymouth's mother had married Papa Price when she was only 14.

"All marriages are not made in heaven," Alice said. "We all have our choices of what we're going to do. Sometimes we make wrong choices."

Alice had always valued education; yet now she was a high school dropout. Her life was all about diapers, dishes, and drab housework. Two years after her daughter was born, Alice gave birth to a son. With two toddlers to feed, she and Weymouth were barely surviving. "My husband was about to starve us to death," she said.

Weymouth and his father tried to mine for coal without joining the union. They were rejected as scabs and shut out. Next Weymouth taught in a one-room schoolhouse heated by a potbelly stove, but his salary was skimpy. Eventually, with Granny babysitting, Alice managed to get her high school diploma. Her teachers taught her typing and shorthand, the gateway skills to a decent secretarial job. Alice pushed Weymouth to move the family to Knoxville in the mountains of Tennessee.

What luck! Bunny Bread hired him to drive a delivery truck. Before long, Alice had landed a clerical job in a doctor's office. Her entire world opened to new possibilities. "I had to learn to drive just to get to work and back," she said.

But she couldn't completely shake the confinement of her former life; on weekends when she and Weymouth returned to Grundy, Papa Price expected them to attend his tent revivals. Papa Price poured himself into his preaching; he slapped his Bible, shouted, and spoke of fire and brimstone. "He was anointed, but he had ignorance," Alice said. "The God he served was a fierce god. He scared people."

What's more, her father-in-law would shame her publicly from the pulpit, criticizing Alice for wearing lipstick or cutting her hair short like a city girl. Everyone would turn and stare. But she put up with it out of respect -- and fear. He didn't hesitate to put them in the hot seat. Once, Alice and Weymouth were sitting on the front row when, from out of the blue, her father-in-law announced that Alice would be up next to sing the day's featured solo. Usually Weymouth's mother warbled a hymn, but she was home sick. Alice was completely unprepared.

Way back in high school, Alice had joined the Methodist church choir, discovering that she made a lovely soprano. But she hadn't sung in the choir for at least a decade. She stood on stage and searched her memory for an appropriate hymn. "I didn't want to embarrass him," she said. After saying a nervous prayer, she managed to remember the words to "I Surrender All".

"God gave me the words, and He gave me the pitch," she recalled. Alice never forgot that moment; from then on, the old hymn would remind her of a rare moment when she had felt loved and protected by the Almighty.

Although Alice had side-stepped a humiliating disaster during the revival, she couldn't overcome the increasing marital difficulties she faced at home. Over time, Weymouth had grown into a caricature of his father. Weymouth imposed harsh household rules, and Alice felt increasingly frustrated. Now that she was working and earning a salary, Alice didn't appreciate her husband bossing her around. "The first one to four years of the marriage were happy and after that it was like, who is this person? I have to stay married to him?" she said.

Alice saw Weymouth as a hypocrite. Despite posturing as a holy roller, Weymouth would sneak into a camping trailer in the back yard to drink, smoke, or rendezvous with a woman he was secretly seeing. Alice had her own distractions. In her spare time, she would go out after work with her friends, smoking and drinking at local honkytonks.

"I wanted to try out my wings," she said. "Weymouth was rebelling a little himself. Both of us were finally acting the way teenagers act, in that stage."

She was in a receptive state of mind when Clint appeared, looking tall, dark, and handsome.

✿ ✿ ✿

Clint had grown up in Lynchburg, VA., the son of a scientist father who had helped develop the atomic bomb for the United States government. After World War II, his family had moved from Washington, D.C. to Lynchburg, where they had settled into a comfortable tree-lined neighborhood. Strong and well-built, Clint was a natural athlete with a knack for tennis. Girls loved him, and he returned their affection. He was an outgoing, good-timing guy. But all was not fun and games for him.

"Clint and his father had a falling out when he was in high

school," Alice said. "His father had met someone else. He tried getting a divorce. He asked Clint to testify against his mother, and he refused."

Clint's father publicly accused his wife of being a drunkard. Clint thought it was a lie. Never would he betray his mother in court. To make matters worse, Clint refused to attend the Virginia Military Institute, the alma mater of his father and grandfather. It was a breach in family tradition when Clint enrolled at the University of Virginia. While there, "Clint was having too much fun," Alice said. "He learned how to shoot beers, chase after the girls, have panty raids, and gamble."

Clint's father was not impressed. After paying for the first two years at UVA, he announced he was through wasting his money. From then on, Clint was left to foot his own bill in life. Clint had to leave the university and his party life behind. Where else to go but back to Lynchburg? Clint found part-time work stringing wire for the telephone company and played team tennis for Lynchburg College while completing his engineering degree. One night he and a girl he'd known since high school got drunk together at a party. It changed his life.

"They drove over to Virginia Beach and got married," Alice said. Three children would come from that union. However, their personalities did not pair well. "Besides being an athlete, Clint was also a social person," Alice said. "Clint was always the life of the party. He loved going to parties, and he loved entertaining. That was not her personality, and they grew in different directions. He liked to have a big time, and he liked to run around."

His wife didn't realize how much running around Clint was actually doing. "Clint would go away to these golf tournaments for the weekend, say over to Greensboro or something, and he would always take a different lady with him," Alice said. Confident as a peacock, Clint had a way of strutting and talking a big game that attracted the opposite sex. Alice had felt his magnetism immediately the day he stepped into her office.

✿ ✿ ✿

After marrying, they moved into a lakeside rental cottage in the Coastal Plains of North Carolina, where Clint worked as an engineer for a textile mill. Two of Alice's three children lived with them in the little town of Riceville, about 50 miles from the beach; Clint's children would visit occasionally from Tennessee, but they resented the presence of their new stepmother.

"They thought they knew that I had taken their father away from their mother," Alice said.

To Alice, the blame was not all hers. Clint's first marriage had been troubled long before she stepped into the mix. To his kids, however, she was the main culprit. "Eventually they stopped visiting," she said.

Despite this, life was exciting for the newlyweds. "The only thing we had in common when we first got married was our sex life," Alice recalled. "It was like we were in heat."

Before long, they fell in with a party crowd. Their merry band of friends would drive 45 minutes over to Myrtle Beach and boogie the night away. Clint mastered the rocking rhythms of the Shag, a popular dance along the Carolina coast, and he could dance for hours at a stretch.

Sometimes Alice would sit down and catch her breath while her hulking husband dipped their female friends around the parquet floor. After sunrise, they'd find a diner, slide into the vinyl banquette seats and load up on coffee, eggs, grits, and bacon. Full of food, they'd drive back in time to make it to work.

Alice clerked in the legal department of a local bank, doing secretarial and administrative tasks. One afternoon Father Billy Walker popped by the bank for an appointment with an executive. Outgoing and loquacious, the priest noticed Alice's mountain twang. His mother's people were mountaineers, and he gabbed all about their part of the Appalachians. Soon they were chatting easily. Alice didn't know him well enough yet to foresee what was coming next.

With Father Billy, the conversation always veered toward Jesus.

"I haven't seen you in church," Father Billy ventured.

"We haven't been," Alice explained.

Father Billy invited her to bring her husband and come to worship at Grace Episcopal Church. Alice didn't get around to visiting. She and Clint were often nursing hangovers on Sunday mornings.

But Riceville was a small town, and before long they met again. Late one night, Alice and Clint were leaving a dance party at the local Country Club as the rector and his wife were going home after dinner with friends. Clint, whose large frame could handle six or seven bourbon highballs, was smashingly drunk.

"You could hear Clint from one end of the ballroom to the other," Father Billy recalled. Father Billy stopped to speak. He introduced his wife, Louise. The priest shook hands heartily with Clint, who was less enthusiastic about the chance meeting. A minute ago, he was having fun; how did he wind up talking to a minister?

Yet the two couples were about the same age, and Father Billy made a mental note to reach out again when everyone was sober. The following Saturday afternoon, the rector showed up uninvited at Alice and Clint's door.

"There's a man out there with a collar on," Clint shouted to Alice. Entertaining a man-of-God was the last thing he wanted, but Clint opened the door and invited the priest inside.

"When I went to call, they had both been drinking all day," Father Billy said. "They were playing pool and cooking spaghetti."

Clint hesitated before offering the preacher a can of beer. Father Billy pulled off the pop-top, took a long sip, and joined them in a round of pool. Clint was relieved. Despite the black shirt and clerical collar, Father Billy seemed ordinary, like someone who could actually be your friend. Clint decided he liked the guy, so on a following Sunday, he and Alice visited Grace Church. Before long, they had even taken a newcomer's class. But their habits remained unchanged — until Alice appeared in danger of dying.

Alice was languishing in the regional hospital over in Wilmington, about 45 minutes away. The cause of her sudden illness remained a mystery; doctors could not find a diagnosis. At the same time, Grace was hosting a revival, and Clint got himself over to the church. Father Billy felt the program was a real challenge for his formal, traditional parish. The guest speaker from Florida preached hard on the need for salvation in Christ and even offered altar calls.

Near the revival's closing service, the guest preacher asked if anyone in the church had an issue he wanted to publicly lay at the feet of Jesus. No one moved, as if scared frozen in the pews. The minister sat down and waited, saying, "Take your time. I've got all night."

To the surprise of all, Clint stood up, towering like a giant at the back of the church.

"You have to understand, Clint was the town reprobate," Father Billy said. "He was known for drinking and whoring. He was the least likely person to show up in church, let alone to stand up in church."

Clint explained that he needed healing for his wife. If she would only get well, Clint would understand that God had done something for him; he promised he would acknowledge and serve God. The next day, Alice's fever broke. Two days later, she was back home.

✿ ✿ ✿

Clint told Alice about his promise. Until then, "we were just pew sitters," Alice said. Eventually, she joined the choir and Clint became a lay reader. They weren't quite ready to give up on the party train, but they were willing to make regular stops at the church.

Along the way, the priest and his wife became close friends to Alice and Clint. The couples developed a rare affection and trust, sharing drinks, meals, and laughter outside the confines of a church relationship.

"They were one of the few couples we've known in 39 years as clergy and spouse who have allowed us to be real," Father Billy confessed. "They put no expectations on us because I was clergy. If I would get mad and yell and scream and throw things against the walls, it would stay with them."

In return, Father Billy offered a new lens for viewing God. "He taught us that Jesus is a savior who loves us," Alice said, "but it never quite got through to me."

Alice struggled to let go of the stern, vindictive images of God from her youth. Deep within her, Alice still carried the shame of being a bastard, of being told that she was not good enough to play with the other children. Also, attending church had made Alice conscious of the fact that she and Clint had sinned when they had abandoned their spouses back in Tennessee.

"In the beginning, we thought it was our right to do that," she recalled. "But then, after we met Billy, the reality hit home that we had broken up two families. I felt very, very guilty about my part in that."

Alice reflected on her faith; it began when she had waded into the cold mountain river for her baptism as a pregnant bride. Although she sincerely believed in God, Alice had chosen to live under the control of her own desires. Now she hungered in her heart to draw closer to God, yet she felt she wasn't pure enough. "In fact, I wasn't sure that I was worthy to go up for Communion," she said.

Several years before Alice left Clint, Father Billy heard her confessions of fear and regret. "He counseled with me about the fact that none of us is worthy to receive Communion, but that Jesus had died so that we could," she said.

After considering these words, Alice allowed herself to return to the Communion table. But she still pulled a wagon of guilt behind her, unsure how to let go. Father Billy's reassurances would come back to her later. Deep change would take time, but the germination process had started in Alice and Clint.

"Father Billy was someone sent by God to work wonders for us," Alice said. "He and Clint just got along."

Sadly, Father Billy received the call to lead a larger church, and eventually he and Louise moved more than four hours away to Elizabeth City, N.C. This was a blow to Clint and Alice. Their faith wasn't deeply rooted yet. Without Father Billy's playful yet protective presence, they fell back in with a crowd of raucous friends. Eventually Alice realized that Clint had committed a few infidelities; well, two could play that game — and she did. They would fight, sometimes separating temporarily.

"They always had an interesting relationship," Father Billy said. "They were never lovey-dovey, sweetie-pie people. They were both feisty people."

Between the drinking and the bickering, Alice and Clint were wallowing in misery. They fell away from attending regular church. Without Father Billy, it wasn't the same. "We let the devil lead us to places we didn't need to be," Alice recalled. Things spiraled downward until she'd had enough. "I decided I was going to try to live the way God wanted me to live instead of the way Alice wanted to live.

❊ ❊ ❊

After Alice left him, Clint turned to Father Billy for support. They spent hours on the phone. "He alternated between languishing or thinking he was better off without her," Father Billy recalled.

One weekend, Clint attended a soul-searching retreat with Father Billy that included a service for spiritual healing. Sunday afternoon, Clint slipped into the private prayer room. There was unrest in his gut; for the first time, Clint had a clear sense of how his self-indulgent life must appear to God.

He poured out his heart in private prayer, confessing all of his faults and misdeeds and begging for another chance. At the retreat's closing ceremony, Clint stood up to speak extemporaneously. In his booming, magnetic voice, he confessed that he was a hard man, a sinner who had driven his wife away, a man of chronic drinking, casual sex, and addictive gambling. And yet, thanks to the work of the Holy Spirit that weekend, he was a new man. He had found peace in the cleansing blood of Christ. The crowd was in awe.

"He was a changed person, no question about that," Father Billy remembered. "Changed does not mean perfect, but he was definitely changed."

Clint called Alice and wanted to take her out to dinner. She left the refuge of the priory and joined him at a table in one of their favorite restaurants. "He said he had laid all his sins in the corner back there," she recalled. "He started confessing his faults and said he would like for us to get back together."

Alice didn't trust him. "I said a leopard will never change his spots," she said. "It's not going to happen."

Her rejection filled Clint with bitterness. Many nasty words would pass between them before all the legal matters of the divorce were finally settled. Eventually, Alice left the monks and moved to be near Judith, her sister, in the mountains of Tennessee. She got an office job; she tried to rebuild her life.

But for what?

She had no husband. Her children were grown and gone. Alice felt like she had no purpose. Her finances were a mess, and her spirit was broken; she was lonely, depressed, and listless. Her daily routine was a bleak cycle of work, household chores, and exercise sessions at her apartment complex's fitness room. She had nothing to look forward to, nothing to inspire her.

Her first Christmas away from Clint was dismal. Clint had always embraced the holiday with his characteristic zest: he made a big deal of cooking the bird, getting up early to pat and rub spices on the turkey, stuffing it, and then baking it to crisp and juicy perfection. Now everything felt stale and flat. The Christmas visits from her children were a nice distraction, but nothing could fill the empty ache.

Alice sank lower on Dec. 29, the day of their wedding anniversary. Was Clint thinking about her? Did he miss her? What was he doing?

"I even called him like a teenager and hung up when he answered," she said. The memory of their bad times "could not kill the love I had for Clint," she said.

Alice had no interest in dating. Once or twice she put herself out there when friends set her up, but she quickly regretted it. Her affections remained tangled up in an impossible, larger-than-life, good looking man, yet Clint appeared gone forever.

"During those two years in Tennessee, I heard nothing from him," she recalled. Then one day, Alice received a long, pleading letter from her ex-husband. Clint had always been a deep sleeper, but he claimed that God had woken him up at 3 a.m. to reveal that their relationship was not finished. They had more pages to write of their story, he said. Clint quoted some Bible passages he had heard at church earlier that week to convince Alice.

"It was a really emotional, moving letter, and it touched my heart," she said. "He said he still loved me, that he had made mistakes, and that he would like for us to try again."

❁ ❁ ❁

Alice was stunned. Her heart pounded and her hands shook as she held onto the letter. Over the next three days, she read Clint's words over and over again. Despite her loneliness, Alice was skeptical. That man could never change. She'd spent 16 years living with him, and she knew him inside and out. She was unwilling to open herself up to more pain.

"But then I thought, are you happy here?" she said. "I decided, not really. When I thought about it, I still felt we were not finished, that things were not complete. I thought I should give it a try."

She, too, had made mistakes; she, too, had regrets. "God was with me and comforted me during my time in the apartment in Tennessee when I was living by myself," she said. "I was just wiped out with fear and love, mainly love for Clint, and I felt that my heart wasn't full because Clint was no longer in it."

She called him. The conversation went surprisingly well. Some of the old feelings, the old chemistry, remained. They agreed to split the driving distance and meet at a Holiday Inn in North Carolina for the weekend. Alice looked younger and better now; during their separation, she had lost weight and updated her hairstyle. Clint had improved too, mainly on the interior.

"I saw a changed man," she recalled. "It wasn't that he had quieted down because Clint was never quiet. He never saw a stranger – he would holler out to people at church. He still had his confidence, his voice. He still loved to dance and to shag, he knew all the moves! But I saw that his mean streak was not there anymore."

After 24 lonely months, Alice now found herself back in Clint's massive embrace, loving him as if her life depended on it. He was voracious and virile as ever, and their physical connection still felt magnetic. When she returned to her apartment in the misty mountains, she missed the sound of his deep voice. She missed his resonating laugh. She even missed the detailed reports about his latest exploits on the golf course.

They started talking regularly over the phone.

A few weeks later, Alice's daughter had a baby, and Alice was heading to Florence, S.C., to help out with laundry, cooking, and newborn care. Clint lived about an hour away, and they quickly agreed that he should drive over for the day. On this second visit, Clint confirmed her hopeful impression.

He was still Clint, but yet, he wasn't. His eyes looked softer, more loving. "I didn't see him making fun of people, saying look at that so-and-so and things like that," she said. "And he listened when we talked together. He just had this love inside him. It was a radical change. I knew that God had taken all the meanness out and replaced it with His love."

Before long, Clint had convinced her to reconcile. "We made plans for me to move back into the house," Alice said.

Against all odds, Clint and Alice had started a brighter chapter of their story.

✿ ✿ ✿

Clint rung up Father Billy to ask if he would re-marry them at his church. By this point, their friend the priest was living over in Sumter, S.C. Father Billy needed to talk to his bishop. The Episcopal

Church did not allow individuals with two strikes against them to marry a third time in its parishes. Soon Father Billy called with happy news: in the church's eyes, Alice and Clint had never divorced, so Father Billy could bless their renewal of vows as man and wife.

"But it wasn't all that easy," Alice said.

"I made them go through hell," Father Billy agreed, laughing. First, he ordered Alice and Clint to set a wedding date several months down the road. Next, the priest told Alice and Clint to quit having sex until after the wedding. Ouch!

In addition, they had to spend a long weekend at the priory, staying in separate cottages and reading selected spiritual texts. After all this, Alice called Father Billy and begged him to move up their wedding date: she and Clint couldn't keep apart much longer. Their friend indulged them, seeing that God was leading them to rejoin their lives.

"Jesus had really softened our hearts," Alice said. "He gave us forgiveness for each other — and for ourselves."

On Nov. 4, 1989, as they married again at Church of Our Savior, Clint and Alice were surrounded by about 500 people, family as well as many new Christian friends. Contemporary praise music set the tone for the upbeat service. Yet during the vows, the bridegroom started to sway and threatened to pass out. He was hung over from going out the night before with friends and his best man, Alice's younger son, Sammy. When Clint's knees buckled, Sammy jumped up behind him and pushed Clint back up, holding a steady hand against his stepfather's back.

"You ain't going nowhere," Sammy said. Clint got through the service.

Afterward, Clint and Alice drove to a cozy mountain cottage for a true second honeymoon. When they arrived, Alice was surprised to see chocolate, roses, and champagne waiting. This was indeed a fresh start. In addition to more patience and tenderness, Clint now had a desire to study the word of God as part of their daily life.

"We would worship together and read the Bible together," Alice says. "Before, we didn't ever open up the Bible." Two years after the wedding, Alice attended the same life-changing Christian retreat where Clint had found freedom from his past.

During the weekend, she experienced a palpable sense of God's presence. "That retreat taught me that God is love," Alice said, "that Jesus loved me warts and all, sins and all. That was when I realized that Jesus loved *me*. Until then, I thought that He loved everybody else, but not me."

Guided by divine love, Alice and Clint did a better job of cherishing each other as man and wife. "They were significantly more forgiving of each other and more willing to work through communication difficulties and issues," Father Billy said. During their second wedding ceremony, Father Billy had offered this counsel: husbands and wives should strive to see Jesus' face when they looked at one another. Those words stuck.

"Clint told me that when they would get feisty, one of them would say, 'I don't see the face of Jesus in you today.' That was enough to get them to see that they weren't handling things the right way," Father Billy said.

❈ ❈ ❈

Clint and Alice shared 24 more years together until he passed away after an extended illness on June 22, 2013. He was 74. His health declined after he contracted a MRSA infection from staying in a local hospital for a routine treatment. While battling MRSA, Clint lost his leg from the knee down. He relied on a wheelchair during his last four years.

Yet ever the athlete, Clint practiced walking with a prosthesis; he worked on his balance, hoping to pick up his golf game again. Sadly, his condition worsened due to leakage in an aortic abdominal aneurysm. His last few months, Clint was weak and housebound. Father Billy still lived in a different city, but he came by and administered last rites over Clint two or three times. Clint crawled back from death's door so many times that Father Billy started calling him

Lazarus.

Clint's impairment hampered him from being able to get out to church, and that really hurt. But for Father's Day 2013, the minister of their local church arranged for a van to carry Clint and Alice to the service. When Clint rolled his chair into the churchyard, so many friends mobbed him that he could hardly get to the front doors.

The homecoming was joyous. "I want to do that more often," Clint told Alice later that day. But the Lord would take Clint before the next Sunday. Alice was by his side when Clint died at home. Although he struggled to breathe, he managed to proclaim his love. He was worried about her.

"I don't want," he whispered, "to leave you here — alone."

Choking back tears, Alice knew she needed to give Clint permission to go. "It's okay," she said, stroking his cheek. "I'm not alone."

As they looked at one another, Clint breathed his last breath, his eyes still locked on Alice's face. Moments later, the finality of their earthly parting registered in her mind; Alice screamed in pain, hardly believing that the love of her life was truly gone.

What was left for her, without Clint?

"If I did not have faith in God and believe in Heaven, I could not endure it," she said. "If I did not know where he is and that I will see him again, I could not survive."

Several years later, Alice is still adjusting to life without him. "It has been an extremely hard thing for me since Clint died," she said. Life will never be the same. Alice occasionally faults herself for not fully recognizing the gift of their togetherness while he was alive.

"Why didn't I tell him how much I appreciated him rolling his wheelchair up and unloading the dishwasher? If only we would have our eyes opened to see what a limited time we have with our loved ones," Alice said.

For the first five months of widowhood, Alice felt stuck, unable to weep, unable to feel, unable to move on; she was vacant, utterly void of all emotions. She reached a turning point one day in the fall when she visited a private chapel where she had an appointment to receive healing prayer. As she knelt with closed eyes, the person leading the prayer service gently asked if she could see the face of Jesus. She tried: in her mind Alice saw the form of Christ, but his face was shadowed. Then suddenly, there was more.

"I see Jesus carrying a heavy adult sheep on his back," she said. What did it mean? Alice was confused. Only as she was driving home did the significance reveal itself: she was the cradled sheep.

"I've got it," she prayed. "You are carrying me now."

The pivotal image of the shooting star returned to her mind. Once again, Alice marveled: God had always taken care of her and guided her, even though she and Clint had committed adultery and broken up their initial marriages. In spite of her sins, God had pursued her. Alice had felt unworthy and unforgivable, and yet, God had forgiven her and helped her to accept freedom from shame.

Despite her mistakes, Alice had received a second chance with Clint when he was a new man. By God's grace, their marriage had blossomed into a beautiful, love-filled relationship for three: man, wife, and Creator.

As a grieving widow, Alice knew that God would continue to walk her through the lonely hours of every day until she saw her beloved Clint again. After experiencing its divine energy in her marriage, Alice understood the power of the resurrection.

❀ ❀ ❀

For Group Discussion

1. Describe what happened when Alice and Clint met. How should a married Christian react when they find themselves feeling drawn to a new person?

2. Did Alice and Clint give much thought to their spouses before launching their affair? What was the immediate result?

3. They didn't try to resist getting involved. Yet what was the cost of their union?

4. How would you describe the lifestyle of the newlyweds? Where do party-oriented marriages usually end up?

5. How did Father Billy work his way into their lives? What impact did the priest have on them?

6. What happened after Clint stood up at the revival and asked for God's help? How did Alice and Clint begin to change after this miracle?

7. What happened after Father Billy and his wife moved to another city? What does this tell you about Alice and Clint's personal relationship with God?

8. How did Alice finally decide that it was right to leave Clint? How can you explain her experience with the shooting star?

9. Alice's departure forced Clint to take stock of himself. What dramatic change happened when Clint went on a weekend retreat with Father Billy?

10. Was Alice right to doubt Clint when he told her that he had changed at the retreat?

11. Alice tried to create a new life for herself, but she was unhappy. What surprising twist happened to Alice after two lonely years of

divorce?

12. What transpired when she and Clint spoke on the phone? What happened when they got together in person?

13. How had they each changed?

14. In the second season of their marriage, what new skills did Alice and Clint employ when they would disagree?

15. What does Alice and Clint's story tell you about God's mercy? About redemption?

16. What finally helped Alice to fully forgive herself?

17. What image did Alice receive to help her during her deep mourning for Clint? Would she have been able to receive this type of reassurance earlier in her life?

18. Despite our feelings of shame or regret, is anyone beyond the help of God? Are we guilty of judging or criticizing others in ways that make them feel unworthy of Christ's friendship?

19. In thinking over the entire story, what was the turning point for Clint? For Alice?

Reflection

"If we confess our sins, He is faithful and just to forgive us our sins and to cleanse us from all unrighteousness."
1 John 1:9

"But this I call to mind, and therefore I have hope: the steadfast love of the Lord never ceases; His mercies never come to an end; they are new every morning. Great is your faithfulness. The Lord is my portion, says my soul. Therefore, I have hope in Him."
Lamentations 3:21-24

Consider how the stigma of Alice's fatherless childhood crushed her feelings of self-worth and clouded her ability to connect with her Heavenly Father. What past hurts or shames may be obstacles for your spiritual growth? Are deep areas of trauma affecting your marriage? Can you trust God enough to let His light shine where you are most vulnerable and tender?

Room for Your Thoughts & Observations

CHAPTER *EIGHT*/Her Tiny Casket

"So, you left the children alone?"

Veronique and Jean were married Nov. 25, 1972

As told by Veronique:

We were young, happy, and in love. After only five years of marriage, Jean and I were thrilled to be surrounded by three lovely little children. We adored our daughter and two sons. God had blessed us with fruitfulness: our babies had been born in rapid succession. As French Catholics, we embraced the idea of having a large family; the youngest child was only seven months old, and I hoped there might be more to come.

Being a wife and mother filled my soul with joy; I felt like the luckiest woman in the world. I had no forewarnings of our loss.

Like most people in Paris, our family lived in a flat. We were on the fourth floor (fifth floor by American standards). Normally it's preferable to find an apartment above the first floor: generally, one gets more air, light, and a better view by moving higher up in the building. Yet looking back now, I would give anything if we had lived on the ground floor.

It happened on a Saturday afternoon; I had gone to Versailles, a town just outside Paris, to attend a drama course. Jean was in charge of the family for a few hours. He was used to having this duty. Everything felt normal when I left for my acting class. Within two hours, the emergency call would come into the drama school.

A secretary interrupted our class and told me: "Your daughter has had an accident." I was to leave immediately and head straight for the children's hospital. I rushed out, hurried into my car, and drove back to Paris, gripping my steering wheel until my knuckles turned white. As a faithful Catholic, I found myself reciting: "Holy

183

Mary, Mother of God, pray for us," over and over.

In less than fifteen minutes, I was in front of the children's hospital. My husband was waiting for me, in tears. What you read about with horror in the newspapers actually happened to us: our daughter Axelle, not quite four years old, had leaned out the kitchen window, lost her balance, and fallen rapidly. She had landed on the pavement below.

Was there any hope? Jean could not bring himself to tell me dreadful news, but by the anguish on his face, I understood. The only words I could utter were, "Can I see her, please?"

We were taken into Axelle's hospital room: a bandage was wrapped around her head. With her babyish cheeks, her innocent expression, and her eyes softly closed, she looked as if she were merely resting tranquilly in the bed. But she had already gone to Heaven. Her lovely face had not suffered in the fall, and she reminded me of a tiny angel. As I gazed at my beautiful young daughter, I thought: her big, expressive eyes have closed forever. Never again will I see that sparkle of merriment in those brown eyes that I love so tenderly. Never again will I hear the joyful music of her carefree giggles.

On that first distressing night at home without Axelle, I didn't sleep a single second. My mind kept replaying the scenes of the day. It wasn't logical, but I yearned to find a way to go back in time and change the sequence of events: if only we had done this or that, could we have saved our precious child from her premature death?

Of course, it was no use, and I was merely torturing myself. Somehow, my husband not only slept, but he snored more loudly than usual. The following night, I didn't feel I could survive listening to Jean snore while I tossed and turned. We are both committed to our faith, so we decided to pray together before going to bed.

A little miracle happened: I was given the grace of falling into the arms of Morpheus without having nightmares. I never had to take any sleeping tablets.

Naturally people wanted to see us to express their compassion. In some way, their kind words were worse than anything for me because they brought my emotions to the surface, and I did not wish to weep in front of my boys. Axelle's brothers were too young to understand what was happening, and I did not want to frighten them by displaying my extreme grief. It's so easy to break down when you keep hearing friends say, "I am so sorry for you, it's unbelievable, she was so sweet...."

At the funeral, many members of our two families, as well as friends and neighbors, had gathered to support us. The church was packed. What amazed me and truly warmed my heart were all the white flowers around and above the small casket of our little daughter. It reminded me of a corner of Paradise. We were seated in the first row, but I was somewhere else ...

It was hard to truly comprehend that this was real. For a few days, I behaved as if I had received the highest dose of anesthesia ever given to any human being. I was living in a state of shock. Everything seemed foggy; my arms and legs felt heavy, and it was hard to think about what I was supposed to be doing.

I couldn't eat much. Nothing felt right.

After ten days under the power of this strange anesthesia, I woke up on the eve of All Saints Day. Toussaint, as we call it in France, is a school holiday around the beginning of November. Jean's sister had kindly invited us to spend several days with her and other family members at her beach house in Brittany. We were happy to get away from our sad apartment. Yet during our stay, something triggered the realization in me that we would never again be a family of five. It was like a bomb, a missile, falling over my skull.

Had I been in my own home, I would have screamed and thrown everything away. Instead, I called out for Jean, my voice shaken with emotion, to join me in private conversation in our bedroom.

For the first time, I asked him for a complete explanation about what had happened on that fateful Saturday.

Perhaps it was the hardest thing he'd ever done, but he told me.

❁ ❁ ❁

All three children had been taking a nap in their beds, and Jean had decided to take advantage of this peaceful time to slip out for a short walk. As he closed the front door, he lingered in the hallway and listened for the sounds of their little voices or feet. No noise. *"They are all fast asleep, I have a few minutes to relax, to breathe the fresh air,"* he thought.

Unfortunately, the quiet did not last. Jean's father came for a visit earlier than expected and rang the doorbell. No one answered. He rang another time. Finally, he heard a few steps behind the door. It was Axelle; she had jumped out of bed and was trying to open the door. However, it was locked. Axelle was very clever, and she tried to do her best. She went into the kitchen and leaned out the window to see who was standing outside the door. As no one was home who could pull her back, she tumbled to her death. Jean's confession shocked me.

"So, you left the children alone, and you didn't think for one second that something could happen?" I asked him. "You went out for a walk, forgetting that your father was coming."

"He was supposed to come later, and I thought I had time," was his poor and miserable answer.

"And leaving the children alone didn't bother you or worry you?" My voice was becoming shrill and charged with anger.

"I know I shouldn't have done it," Jean muttered.

I didn't have the energy to drag out this painful cross-examination, especially in a cottage filled with Jean's extended family; I had heard enough. I fled to the beach alone, where I walked and walked and cried as much as I could. I asked God and Mother Mary for help. Would I ever be able to forgive Jean? His faulty judgment had caused the death of our beloved Axelle. It was too hard, too heavy a burden for a young mother like me. Our future together as husband and wife was completely unclear.

What were we going to do? What, what?

When I had exhausted all my tears, I returned to the beach house. Everyone was gathered in the den. One of our nieces was making Remi, our two-year-old, laugh. Hearing his giggle felt like a temporary balm on my wound. At last, he was having fun again.

I knew Remi missed his sister. Axelle had always played with him and been his leader. He did not even understand where she had gone. Everything was a reminder of Axelle's absence.

I pretended to be fine, but my facial expressions gave me away. I could not look at my husband without wanting to explode. Everyone sensed that something serious had happened between Jean and me. They had probably been dreading this moment.

One of my husband's sisters approached me privately. In a kind voice, she said: "You know, Jean suffers too."

I knew what she meant. Of course, Jean was suffering from guilt and remorse as well as loss. As a sister, she wanted to protect her brother, feeling that a war was about to break out between us. Yet her words made me furious; I needed comfort, not advice. I was too weak emotionally at that time to offer forgiveness to my husband for his monumental mistake.

My eyes filled with tears, yet I didn't answer her. How could I? Despite her nudging, I still couldn't bring myself to let go of my resentment. It was too much even to talk with Jean; I could only exchange the minimum words needed to take care of Remi and baby Matthew. A chasm of heartsickness separated us.

Time slowed to a crawl. One day felt as long as a week for me. I missed my daughter so much that I thought I might die of a broken heart in order to join her. Wanting to help, Jean's sister encouraged us to stay at the beach until the end of the week. We accepted. We were in no hurry to return to Paris and face the emptiness created by the departure of Axelle.

When the week ended, it was bitterly hard to leave. After a moving goodbye of hugs and tears, we withdrew from the supportive circle of Jean's family. Once again, I felt the reality of our staggering loss: someone pivotal was absent from our hearts and our home, and there was nothing Jean nor I could do to change that. Life was forcing us to move on, and now the remaining four of us were standing in front of our destiny. Somewhere in my mind, I managed to think about the future.

"Am I going to stay mute with my husband for the rest of my

life?" I whispered to myself.

How cheerful that would be for all of us! I didn't want to live that way, but I was frozen emotionally. I had only one motive in mind, to keep the rest of my family safe and in good health: my husband, Remi, and Matthew, a cheerful baby who was always smiling. I carried on with my work like a robot. In moments of desperate prayer, I begged God and Mother Mary to help me forgive my children's father.

It hardly seemed possible.

Yet God heard my pleas, and He touched me. After several more days of cold silence toward my husband, I felt something lift within my soul. I had received clarity: I could choose to harbor bitterness and anger, but in doing so, I would lose my marriage as well as my daughter. "Jean, I want to talk to you again," I uttered one afternoon.

Surprised, he turned his head towards me.

"Please, let us try to stay close to each other, because I need you, and you need me, and the children need us both," I said. Jean didn't say a word, but his gaze was filled with such deep tenderness that I reached out and squeezed his hand.

"Shall we go into the garden, all together?" I suggested. He nodded with relief.

Moments later, we ventured out with Remi and played with a big rubber ball. Little Matthew joined us from his pram, smiling as usual. We were still a family, and we had to trim the sail, pushed by a wind coming from Heaven, from God who offers His help whenever we suffer. Our little daughter was physically gone, but she remained hidden in our hearts, playing her part from Heaven.

The four of us spent the rest of the week linked together, bearing our grief in quiet companionship. Jean and I didn't feel the need to discuss what had happened. But we had the very good fortune of sharing the same faith. We entrusted our relationship to the Holy Virgin, and every night we recited prayers together on our rosary. The daily reminder of her selfless love and immense compassion helped me to throw away the negative thoughts which had threatened to poison our marriage.

Let your family be wrapped under the coat of the Holy Virgin.

I cherished these words, written to me from a beloved prioress at a convent where my sister was a nun. In my mind, I visualized this comforting image, praying repeatedly for the Mother of God to cover us with her cloak of mercy and grace.

Hard as it was, our life together had to be rebuilt. You can't leap ahead with giant steps, but you can still tread forward in forgiveness if you are well surrounded by the love of God. That is exactly what happened.

Axelle died on Oct. 22; the next year, on the 20th of October, we were blessed with the birth of little Raphael. I didn't realize it until after we had named him, but in Hebrew, Raphael means *God heals.*

Each child has his own place in a family, and you will never re-place the child who is gone forever. No matter how much time passes, you will never forget. But with the presence of God, the ten-derness of the Holy Virgin, and the inspiration of the Holy Spirit, you can convert your pain into acceptance and refill your heart with hope and confidence. We will never stop missing Axelle, but Jean and I trust that we will see her again. And by God's grace, her loss did not destroy our love for one another.

❀ ❀ ❀

For Group Discussion

1. What was Veronique's life like before the tragedy?

2. After seeing her daughter's body at the hospital, how did Veronique respond?

3. Why didn't she press her husband for more details regarding the accident?

4. What happened at home that night on her first evening without Axelle? Why did Jean's snoring bother Veronique?

5. Instead of taking a sleeping pill, what did Veronique do on the second night to help herself before she went to bed?

6. What was Veronique's experience during the funeral?

7. At first, Veronique was in a daze. What happened when she her mind cleared, and she became lucid again?

8. What did Jean confess to Veronique about the details of the tragedy? How did she respond to the news that her husband had left the children home alone?

9. Have you ever had to deal with a situation where someone's mistake led to the death or trauma of a loved one? How did you handle this?

10. Who did Veronique turn to for help as she walked along the beach and cried in grief?

11. How did Veronique feel about Jean when she returned to the beach house? Do you think Jean's sister was right to speak to Veronique about forgiving her husband? How did her words affect Veronique?

12. It is not uncommon for parents to divorce after the death of a child. What can be done when "a chasm of heartsickness" separates

a married couple?

13. Why did Veronique feel like a robot when the family returned home to Paris and carried on with their daily life?

14. What was her constant prayer?

15. How did God answer her prayer? What clarity did Veronique receive and how did it change her attitude?

16. How did Jean respond when she reached out to him?

17. How did their common faith help Jean and Veronique move forward?

18. Turning her thoughts to the Virgin Mary gave courage to Veronique. What aspect of God or person of the Holy Trinity is most comforting and approachable to you?

19. The power of positive thought and visualization can move mountains. How did Veronique use this resource to strengthen her faith?

20. What is significant about the name Raphael?

21. Why are so many people unable to forgive after a tragedy? What was the turning point for Veronique?

Reflection

"The Lord is near to the brokenhearted and saves the crushed in spirit."
Psalm 34:18

"He will wipe every tear from their eyes. There will be no more death or mourning or crying or pain, for the old order of things has passed away."
Revelation 21:4

Jean's sister tried to soften Veronique's resentment of her husband before the grieving mother could come to terms with her loss. When someone is in great pain, words of advice can feel like a slap in the face.

Try to remember a time when you needed empathy, and someone attempted to fix you with unwanted advice or a quick solution. What wounded people most need is reassurance that tomorrow will be brighter, especially if they surrender themselves – and their troubles – into God's loving care. Look for opportunities to extend understanding to those who are hurting, regardless of who is to blame. By simply listening without judgment, you can help a friend work through her thoughts and emotions. Feeling heard goes a long way toward helping someone survive a difficult situation.

Room for Your Thoughts & Observations

CHAPTER *NINE* / Asked to Forgive

"I found myself wanting revenge."

Rebecca and George married in 1992; they separated in 2008 and divorced in 2009.

As told by Rebecca:

It began with a chance encounter. My husband, George, and I were considering moving to a coastal town. In truth, we had hit some bumps in our marriage; we'd considered separating, but we did not want to do that to our kids. We decided to move to a charming community along the Sea Islands of Georgia, to slow down the pace of our lives, and to throw ourselves into strengthening our relationship.

Before long, I met a lovely real estate agent in the new area who seemed able to help us; Karen was blonde and warm, and her smile was filled with Southern hospitality. We closed on a house, moved before school started, and began the process of getting acclimated. Our family easily adapted to the laid-back pace of life at the beach, and I felt certain that George and I had begun a happy new chapter together.

Soon Karen was more than our Realtor; she became a close family friend. She and her husband Steve lived in our new neighborhood. Their oldest girl was the same age as our youngest son. The kids got along, and this helped cinch our families together.

A year and half later, my husband and I decided that we needed a larger home. Naturally, we contacted Karen and enlisted her help. We viewed many homes as we leisurely looked. Nothing on the market tempted us. Then we learned about a house that might be *the one*. It was about to go on the market. Karen took us on a tour of the house. We loved it and made an offer that day.

In the following months, George and I were in constant contact with Karen. There was a mounting excitement. We closed in November and began work on the hardwood floors and painting the interior. We decided to move in after Christmas and New Year's Eve.

The move was uneventful, and we placed our former home on the market. Karen went to work for us once more.

January turned into spring. Something was wrong with my husband. George was under a lot of pressure at a new job. He seemed distant, but our kids' activities kept us busy.

I had hope for our upcoming family vacation where we were traveling with fourteen families to the Bahamas. After a particularly fun couples-only evening where George and I had danced and laughed, we held hands as we made our way back to our rental house. After checking on the kids, I fell asleep as soon as my head touched the pillow. Too much sun, alcohol, and dancing had made it impossible for me to stay awake.

The next morning, George expressed his dissatisfaction. I was told that we no longer wanted the same things and that he was going back to the States that day and wanted a divorce. I was in shock. I was humiliated, terrified, and heartbroken. Several days later, the kids and I had to make our way back home on our own.

When we arrived, George had moved into the guest room and was making arrangements to move into our previous house, which was still on the market. I was confused. I had not seen this coming. George wouldn't discuss it.

Our marriage was over.

❁ ❁ ❁

After two weeks, George admitted he was having an affair. I guessed that it was his personal trainer. He did not correct me. Sadly, such betrayal was old territory for me.

When I was sixteen, my dad had left my mother for another woman. It had been devastating for my mother, sister, and me.

Sitting in a darkened hallway, listening to my mother cry in her room for two weeks, I promised myself -- no man would ever have that kind of power over me. Subconsciously, I built a wall around my heart, although for many years I was not aware that it existed. During my marriage with George I recognized the self-made barrier, but I could not figure out how to bring it down.

Several years earlier, when I felt a lack of intimacy in my marriage that I could not fix, I had pleaded with God to bring down this protective wall, no matter what. Two weeks after my petition, I discovered that George had dabbled in an affair with a colleague at work.

Instantly, the wall around my heart collapsed, as I felt raw with pain. I cried for 36 hours. I realized that the wall had actually hindered my relationships. George and I worked hard to get past his unfaithfulness, prompting our move to the beach.

George saw his affair as a result of my inadequacies; sadly, I bought into his assessment. I worked harder on myself and our marriage to prove that I was worthy.

This mindset originated during my father's betrayal of my mother. In a matter of days, I went from being the apple of my father's eye to having to prove myself to him. The transition was too much for a sixteen-year-old to master. My relationship with my father became a casualty of their divorce.

During my teens and early adulthood, God was my constant. When I turned to Him, He was there. He became my Father, and at times I would call Him Abba or even Daddy. When I struggled with my relationship with my stepmother, He was there. When boyfriends broke my heart, He was there. In the still of the night, He comforted me. When I called out to Him, peace would wash over me and give me strength.

Years later, after turning forty, I went through a year of doubting God, yet my faith had come back stronger. Now here I was in my mid-forties, learning for the second time that George had been sexually involved with another woman. This time, George wasn't willing to discuss reconciliation. He was done.

After my husband's first affair, I had felt God leading me to forgive George and save our marriage; I tried that and now I was in the midst of a terrible divorce. I questioned God's intentions. Why did I have to go through this?

✿ ✿ ✿

The next several months would require deep soul searching. For starters, I spent time jogging along a path that bordered the marsh near my home. This daily exercise became an act of survival; I needed a way to get stress out of my body. Often, I was praying and crying as I ran. I did not want to admit to myself, or George, that once again he was right. I was the messed up one.

Following God's nudging, I went away for help while my kids were at summer camp. Thankfully George agreed to pay for my much-needed support. First, I spent a week attending a therapeutic group session at a treatment center, working through old wounds from my childhood. There was healing, camaraderie, compassion, and laughter in my group. The therapists led us in exercises that allowed me to see myself in new ways.

After that, I spent an additional week at a beautiful wellness retreat in Mexico where I invested many hours in quiet reflection. As I sat and listened for inner guidance, God revealed that I was in the process of becoming a butterfly. I was a caterpillar, about to go through the painful metamorphous where everything inside me would be reconfigured. God promised that upon emerging from this transformation, I would be a beautiful creature, able to soar.

I returned home feeling renewed. I had a long way to go before I was healed, but the process had begun. I picked up the kids from camp, feeling hopeful and happy to see them. We had just gotten in the front door of my house when George appeared.

There was something he had to tell me. From his serious tone, I knew that I was not ready to hear whatever it was. I had traveled many hours that day. I ached for a good night's sleep. He insisted that we needed to talk.

Sitting outside on our porch, listening to the rain on the tin roof, I heard George confess that he was having an affair with Karen — my very first friend here. The neighborhood already knew. They had gotten caught while I was away, and he knew I would hear about it in the morning. He wanted to control my response. He was worried about Karen and what Steve would say.

I was in shock. I had trusted them as we bought two houses together. Even though my husband's betrayal ran deeper, hers had broken the bonds of sisterhood. I felt even more humiliated and worthless now that I knew that Karen, my close and trusted friend, was the other woman. This would explain why she had seemed a bit distant lately. What a fool I had been for not picking up on any of this!

I ran from the porch to get away from his confession. I sprinted for over a mile as the rain mixed with my tears. How could they do this to me, a good and loving person? Would this pain never end? "God, where are you?" I yelled into the night. He did not answer. I felt abandoned in the deepest recesses of my being. It was the beginning of the dark night of my soul.

Because of the intense emotional pain, I knew I was susceptible to misusing alcohol. God gave me the image of my children having to pick me up on a golf cart at a neighborhood bar, drunk. I could not do that to them. I decided to stop drinking. At a time when I desired to be numb and forget my circumstances, even for a moment, I needed to be sober and strong.

✿ ✿ ✿

I am not a vengeful person, but I found myself wanting revenge. I had trusted Karen as our real estate agent; yet she had taken George into houses alone, creating opportunities for their secret liaisons.

Karen's behavior was grossly unprofessional; she should not be able to get away with this. For weeks, I entertained ways of getting even. I called the National Association of Realtors, gave the broadest details of the situation, and asked if I had a case. Could I file for disbarment? I was told that I did have a case and how to proceed.

I imagined the destruction I could inflict on her. Of course, George was also to blame, but in my mind, Karen morphed into the destroyer of my marriage. I wanted her to suffer like I was suffering. By exposing and shaming Karen, I would also inflict punishment on George.

In the midst of my temper tantrum, God showed me who I would become if I went down that path. I would no longer be innocent. My children would hear of my actions and have to choose sides. I would jeopardize my relationship with God. In taking matters into my own hands, I was showing that I did not trust Him.

I struggled. I wanted justice, but was retribution mine to inflict? I was reminded of Romans 12:19, a warning against hurting others out of spite. "Vengeance is mine, I will repay, says the Lord."

My faith began to surface. I went back to my core values. I received clarity: to extract vengeance on Karen would fundamentally change who I was as a person, and I would not like the end result. I handed God my yearning for justice, and He accepted.

✿ ✿ ✿

Yet every time I felt myself beginning to feel stronger, I was confronted with a new situation that knocked me back down. I started seeing Karen in random places. As I entered our neighborhood after a morning of running errands, she walked right across the street. Everywhere I turned, Karen seemed to be there. My friends were spooked by my constant sightings of the other woman. What was going on?

At times, I felt my sanity slip. One particular morning, I dropped off my kids at school and drove to our old house. George was living there, and Karen was often with him. This time, I wanted to confront her. Her Volvo SUV was parked in front. Good! This was still my house. How dare she!

I rang the doorbell once, twice, keeping my finger on the buzzer. I wanted to see her face. George answered and let me in. He said that she would not come down. I stood at the bottom of the steps, yelling slut and whore. In a moment, I came awake, witnessing myself acting in this awful manner. I took deep breaths and walked out of the door. I got into my car, ashamed of my behavior.

Time passed, and God gave me the strength to meet the pain and better deal with it, even as George and Karen became engaged and eventually married. George and I shared joint custody, so our kids split time between two households. Likewise, Karen had joint custody of her daughters. She and George began to build a Brady Bunch family — with *my* children. Karen was acting like a fairy Godmother to my kids; I felt as if she was trying to steal my children as well as my husband. For example, Karen took my preteen daughter shopping to buy her first bra. I was furious that she had snatched that moment away from me.

Weeks later, I was still upset about the shopping incident when I bumped into George and Karen; they were sitting in George's truck when I drove up to a friend's house to pick up our son from a playdate. Seeing them together set me off. I confronted George, and he got out of the truck. I was shaking uncontrollably. I screamed up at his face, and I screamed at Karen through the closed window. I felt out of control. Some corner of my brain told me to calm down, that our son watching, but I could not stop myself.

I realized that I needed help. I began working with a Christian counselor and also meeting with a mentor. This helped, but even so, I continued to carry around the desire for justice. I asked God when He would defend me and my good name. Where was He when George and Karen appeared to be living life to the fullest? They were in bliss, and I was mired in pain. They were reveling in their new romantic adventure, and I was alone.

In the quiet of my mind, God's response surprised me. He cut straight to the point: they would not experience the consequences until I no longer cared. I had to stop wanting justice. He didn't want me to rejoice in their downfall. In His great wisdom, God valued the condition of my heart and knew if I was locked on revenge, I would not be ready for the future He had planned for me.

Wait, I had to stop caring if they suffered consequences? When I had placed my desire for revenge in God's hands more than a year ago, I did not know this was the deal.

"Daddy, I want justice."

"Daughter, I want your heart."

I started to cry. He was right. My heart was more valuable than any vengeful act. As crazy as it seemed, God was leading me to consider forgiving the object of my deepest anger: Karen.

❀ ❀ ❀

In the months ahead, I embarked on a mission to define what forgiveness was and what it was not. I had done my best to dredge up forgiving Karen with my head, asking God to help me make it real. Despite this, I felt His presence asking for something deeper, something that would release me from this spiritual swamp.

I had discussed this with my mentor, and she had assured me that God would show me the way if I was willing. I was desperate for relief, so I told God, "OK, you win. I'll do whatever."

Several weeks later, God would push me to act on this. It happened on a hot August day; my time of custody was starting again, so I drove over to George and Karen's house.

As many times as I had picked up and dropped off my kids, I had never walked up the front steps. My usual pattern was to text my kids when I arrived. I would focus on the house across the street until my kids got into my car. It was just too awkward and painful. The few times I found myself looking at their house, I was stunned all over again that I was the outsider.

This time, the circumstances of pickup would run differently. A couple of blocks from their house, God said, "Today is the day."

Whoa. I pulled my car closer to the curb.

"What do you mean, Lord?"

"Today is the day."

I sensed He was talking about my extending forgiveness to Karen. "No, please, I'm not ready. How can it be the day? I don't know what to say."

"Today is the day," continued to flow through my mind. I felt anxiety rise within me. I sat, staring out the front window. He would not let it go.

"Ok." I offered, wanting to obey, but not fully able to agree. "I'll speak to her if she's there." I began to breathe deeply, calming myself with the knowledge that Karen would likely be at work. Comforted by my logic, I drove toward their house. My heart sank. Karen's Volvo was parked in the driveway.

I sat there staring at their house.

"Go to the front door," I felt God prompt me.

"What? I've never gone to their front door. How can you ask this of me?"

"Go to the front door," He repeated.

Now I was resentful. He was pushing me too far! Like an annoyed teenager, I slammed the driver's door as I exited the car. I marched toward the house and stomped up the steps. Now what? I held my fist a foot away from the door, hesitating, hoping God would let this test pass me. When He remained quiet, I released the power behind my fist and banged a couple times.

Nothing.

Again, I banged. Again, quiet. I waited for five minutes.

Nothing.

I skipped down the steps, immense relief coursing through me. Okay, so it looked like God had only wanted me to be willing. I had done it. That was enough.

I jumped in my car and immediately texted my kids that I was waiting for them.

But He wasn't satisfied. "Text her."

"God, you're asking too much from me. I was willing at the door. I don't want to text her."

I sat there wanting to cry. "Please Daddy, don't make me do this. I can't."

"Text her."

I looked at the screen of my phone, pulled up her number and began.

I am outside. Do you have a minute to talk?

Is this meant for me? She was smart to ask. In three and a half years, I had only texted her twice, and both of those times had been a mistake.

I began typing, *Yes, it is for you,* but I hesitated to send the reply.

Part of my brain was in shock that I was actually doing this; was I losing my mind? However, my job was to obey the Holy Spirit, even if His directions made no sense at that moment. Taking a deep inhale, I pushed send. I sat there, stunned, not knowing how this was going to play out. I didn't know what I was going to say because I did not want to talk to her.

Moments later, my three children bounded through the front door. I stepped from my car to hug them. Karen's daughters followed on their heels; I said a polite hello. Next George appeared, standing next to our children. My heart sank. I hadn't known he was home.

I asked God, "How's this going to work?" Then I added, "This is all you, Daddy. I'm just here for the ride."

With a slight shake of my head, I glanced over and saw Karen coming out of the door. She joined us in a semi-circle around my car. The kids' energy gave me strength as the summer sun beat down. I started to sweat.

My children ran into the house to get their stuff. Her daughters went off to play. George disappeared and all of a sudden, she and I were alone. "Do you mind if we walk down the street to that shade?" I asked, pointing to a large shadowed area on the asphalt. "Ok," she answered. We walked side by side without speaking.

My mind was utterly blank.

As we moved underneath the overhanging branches of the large oak tree, we turned to face each other. We were within a foot of one another. I looked into her eyes and saw sadness. I was shocked. Looking at them from the outside, Karen and George seemed like the perfectly happy couple. Now I saw that she was hurting, too.

I opened my mouth, hesitating for a moment, "I forgive you for everything you have done to me, and I ask you to forgive me for the times I was unkind." I said it quickly, in one breath.

She and I were both stunned by my words. I watched her eyes tear up. "How can I not forgive you when you are forgiving me for far more?" Karen said.

Her tears started to flow, and to my shock, I witnessed her anguish, mixed with shame. I could no longer hate her. All along, I had seen myself as the victim, and yet God wanted me to witness the bigger picture. On some level, Karen was tormented by what she had done, and her guilt was eating away at her.

We spoke for twenty minutes with tears running down both of our faces. We even hugged. As I got into my car, I felt a weight being lifted. Our friendship was forever lost, yet I was finally at peace. At last I understood: God loves us equally. Karen is His precious child, too.

❈ ❈ ❈

Months went by, and I felt much lighter in my heart. I had done what God had asked me to do. I felt free. To my great surprise, I would soon learn that Karen and George were having marital issues of their own. After several years of marriage, they split up. By God's grace, I kept myself from gloating.

About six months into their separation, Karen sent me a text. She wanted me to know: my example of offering costly forgiveness was giving her strength in her own divorce process. Now Karen felt that she should apologize to me in person. Could she contact me when she was ready?

"Sure," I said, "let me know and we can get together." I knew I needed to allow her that closure. Another six months passed before

I received a text. We agreed upon breakfast a couple days later. I faced her, this time sitting in a cafe. With tears in her eyes, she asked for my forgiveness. I assured her that she was forgiven.

I asked her if she regretted losing our friendship. She said that I would never know the extent of her regret. At that moment, I missed our friendship and was sad that she was experiencing pain. Even though she had brought it upon herself, I didn't feel any satisfaction.

Our breakfast turned into lunch as we sat at an outdoor table. The sun's shadows slowly moved across our table as our water glasses were filled over and over. We talked about misunderstandings, sadness, and happier times. We refrained from speaking about the man who had come between us. We focused on what the future held for each of us.

Six hours later, we parted with a deep and sincere hug. For me, it was finally and fully over. God had given me the opportunity to surrender and to heal my heart. In the healing, He was setting me up for the next chapter of my life.

❀ ❀ ❀

For Group Discussion

1. How had infidelity been a problem in Rebecca and George's marriage in the past? Why did Rebecca place much of the blame on herself?

2. At their Bahamas vacation, when George told Rebecca that he wanted a divorce, what was her reaction? Was George willing to discuss ways of saving their marriage? What would you do if you were suddenly plunged into this situation?

3. How did Rebecca feel when she learned the truth about her friend Karen? Why did this increase her feelings of betrayal and anger? Do you think she was angrier at Karen than at George?

4. In the first six months to a year following the separation, what positive things did Rebecca do to help herself cope? How did she lean into her faith?

5. Rebecca considered reporting Karen to the national board of Realtors. How was her desire for revenge changing her at a core level? What helped her to recognize the danger of exacting revenge?

6. For many months, George and Karen were in bliss, while Rebecca was tormented by frequent sightings of her nemesis. Rebecca felt Karen was even trying to win over her children by playing fairy godmother to them. How did Rebecca feel about herself after she unleashed her fury on Karen and George?

7. With professional help, Rebecca worked hard to forgive, yet she sensed any progress was limited to her head. She was still anxious for God to defend her and exact vengeance. What was she expecting from God?

8. Instead, what promise did Rebecca receive from her Heavenly

Father concerning George and Karen, and herself?

9. What did God tell Rebecca about the condition of her heart? How did this give Rebecca strength and hope?

10. Eventually Rebecca sensed that she was being called to forgive Karen. Did this seem possible? Why did Rebecca agree to obey?

11. How did Rebecca know when the time came for her to act out her forgiveness? What was Rebecca's attitude toward God as she texted Karen and rang the doorbell at the happy couple's new house?

12. Like Rebecca, would you be able to follow the inner voice and go out on a limb to obey God? Why or why not?

13. To her amazement, Rebecca heard herself granting forgiveness to the woman who had stolen her husband. What did Rebecca learn about Karen by her reaction?

14. How did the tears streaming down Karen's face help Rebecca see the other woman, not as an enemy, but as a person in deep pain?

15. How did Rebecca feel after this dramatic encounter? What surprising news did she receive several months later?

16. How was Rebecca a role model for Karen? Was Rebecca sincerely able to offer Karen total forgiveness when she asked for it? What did that do for both of them?

17. What did Rebecca gain from this quest to forgive? In what way were her children protected by her hard work to surrender her need for revenge? How did this work enable Rebecca to move on with her life?

18. In thinking back over the story, what was the turning point for Rebecca?

Reflection

"For if you forgive other people when they sin against you, your heavenly Father will also forgive you. But if you do not forgive others their sins, your Father will not forgive your sins.
Matthew 6:14-15

"Get rid of all bitterness, rage and anger, brawling and slander, along with every form of malice. Be kind and compassionate to one another, forgiving each other, just as in Christ, God forgave you."
Ephesians 4:31-32

Search your heart to see if you are holding onto grudges or resentments. Sit quietly with whatever comes up and offer it up to God, asking Him to show you how to begin letting go. Take whatever steps He suggests, trusting that you are on the path toward inner healing and recovery. Understand that forgiveness is a process, and trust in the Lord to lead you there with perfect timing.

Sometimes keeping a journal of your progress toward forgiveness provides a safe place to pour out your feelings. Also, as you look back over earlier passages, you will see how far you have come and remember the many ways in which the Lord provided assistance along the way.

Room for Your Thoughts & Observations

If You're Wondering....

Rebecca brought her story to me after the first edition of this book was published. That edition had eight chapters, each about a saved marriage. After the book was released, many divorced Christians told me that they wished they had found this book earlier, while they were still married. "It might have made a difference," they'd suggest. Many had hoped to save their marriage, but their spouse was determined to check out of the relationship.

Unless both partners are willing to surrender to God, reconciliation and intimacy will prove elusive. This last chapter offers a wonderful picture of the faithfulness and tender mercies of our Heavenly Father in leading Rebecca from brokenness, following her unwanted divorce, back to wholeness.

Take heart, woman or man of God. No matter what happens in your life, even if others abandon or disappoint you, the Lord will never leave you.

About the Author

Pringle Franklin, former correspondent for *The Kansas City Star,* is a freelance writer and Christian blogger. She used her journalism skills for this collection. Her second book, <u>Your Forever Friend</u>, released in 2017, is a Christian memoir about the life of the late Preston Hipp of Charleston, S.C. Ms. Franklin is a veteran Bible study and discussion group leader for women. She leads a weekly Centering Prayer group at her church. Her inspirational video interviews are available on YouTube on the Pringle Franklin channel. Ms. Franklin also writes poetry for young children. She has been married to Dr. Sam Franklin since 1991 and is the mother of three sons, Clay, Benton, and Baker Franklin.